101 Tips for Online Course Success:

An online course companion and daily planner

Randy Nordell

American River College

101 TIPS FOR ONLINE COURSE SUCCESS: AN ONLINE COURSE COMPANION
AND DAILY PLANNER

Published by McGraw-Hill Education, 2 Penn Plaza, New York, NY 10121. Copyright © 2015 by
McGraw-Hill Education. All rights reserved. Printed in the United States of America. No part of this
publication may be reproduced or distributed in any form or by any means, or stored in a database or
retrieval system, without the prior written consent of McGraw-Hill Education, including, but not limited
to, in any network or other electronic storage or transmission, or broadcast for distance learning.

Some ancillaries, including electronic and print components, may not be available to customers outside
the United States.

This book is printed on acid-free paper.

1 2 3 4 5 6 7 8 9 0 DOC / DOC 1 0 9 8 7 6 5 4

ISBN   978-0-07-802092-6
MHID   0-07-802092-1

Senior Vice President, Products & Markets: *Kurt L. Strand*
Vice President, Content Production & Technology Services: *Kimberly Meriwether David*
Director: *Scott Davidson*
Executive Director of Development: *Ann Torbert*
Development Editor: *Allison McCabe*
Executive Marketing Manager: *Keari Green*
Director, Content Production: *Terri Schiesl*
Content Project Manager: *Rick Hecker*
Senior Buyer: *Debra R. Sylvester*
Design: *Jana Singer*
Cover Image: *Kyoshino/Getty Images*
Senior Content Licensing Specialist: *Jeremy Cheshareck*
Typeface: *10/11 Times LT Std*
Compositor: *Laserwords Private Limited*
Printer: *R. R. Donnelley*

www.mhhe.com

Table of Contents

PART 1: PREPARING BEFORE THE COURSE BEGINS

Since you are enrolled in and taking classes at college, you want to do as many things as possible to ensure your success. Although your classes will vary, there are many things you can do to help you be successful in college.

1 Meet with an Academic Counselor

Academic counselors are a wealth of knowledge about not only classes, majors, and degrees but also college support services, financial aid, job search services, and internships and work experience. Your counselor might not be able to answer all questions you might have, but they can usually point you in the right direction and get you to the person who can answer your questions.

When you begin college, you should meet with an academic counselor to create an academic plan to help you reach your educational goals. Once your academic plan is in place, meet with a counselor at least once a year to review your plan and make adjustments as needed. Following is a list of questions you might ask, and you'll probably have many others. Write down questions as you think of them so you remember to ask your counselor.

- Which campus support services are available?
- Is financial aid available for me?
- How do I get tutoring if I need it?
- Am I taking the classes I need to graduate on time according to my academic plan?
- What happens if I drop a class or if I don't pass a class?
- How do I change my major?
- Is the finals schedule different from the regular class schedule when taking an online course?

2 Learn Which Support Services Are Available at Your School

Most campuses have many resources to assist you in your education. Take time to find out what these resources are before the term begins. If you know what is available to help you succeed, you are able to take advantage of these resources as the need arises. Some of the possible educational resources that might be available include:

- Library and resource librarians
- Counselors

1

- Instructional technology center (help with computer issues)
- Computer labs
- Writing, reading, math, and science labs and support services
- Disabled student services
- Tutoring center and tutors
- Career center
- Assessment or testing center
- Veterans' services
- Re-entry services
- Business services and administration and records

Many of these services offer workshops throughout the term such as "Resume Writing" or "Research Techniques." Look up dates of workshops that are of interest to you and put these dates on your calendar. At many campuses, emails are regularly sent to all students with information about upcoming workshops.

3 Apply for Financial Aid

It is always a good idea to apply for financial aid when attending college. Even if you don't think you qualify, take the time to go through the application process and see if you are eligible for financial assistance to help pay for tuition and book costs.

All schools have a financial aid office that can provide you with an application package, deadlines, and help in completing the application. ***Make sure you get your application in by the deadline.*** The lack of ability to purchase textbooks before the term begins negatively influences student success. This is sometimes due to students not meeting the financial aid deadlines, which causes a delay in disbursements and delays the ability to purchase textbooks.

Also, make sure you complete and update your FAFSA (Free Application for Federal Student Aid) information yearly and by the due date. Your school has information about FAFSA, and this information can be found online (**www.fafsa.ed.gov**).

4 Get Your Books and Supplies Early

One of the most effective ways to get off to a good start in your classes is by purchasing the books, other supplementary resources, and supplies early. Most professors have the textbook and supplementary materials selected months before the term begins, and these materials are usually listed on the professor's web site, college bookstore web site, or course schedule.

Getting your books and supplies early not only makes you more prepared, but you also avoid the last minute buying rush, shipping delays, and the possibility of the book being sold out. By starting early, you have time to search for the best price on your textbook. Textbooks are expensive, and you can save money by searching for the best prices through online textbook retailers such as Amazon and Barnes and Noble. You can also rent textbooks or buy an e-book version as a cost-saving alternative.

5 Get the Syllabus Early and Read through it

For online and hybrid courses, the course syllabus is your road map. The syllabus lists the professor's contact information, course materials, course requirements, grading standards, and the schedule of assignments. The course syllabus is usually available on the professor's web site or learning management system (LMS).

It is important to get the syllabus early and review it carefully. As you review the syllabus, look for the following:

- What is the best way to contact the professor?
- What are the instructor's expectations of you?
- How are you being graded?
- How are assignments submitted?
- How are tests taken?
- What are the important due dates?
- Are there group projects?
- Are there online learning resources to help you?

As you review the syllabus, you will undoubtedly have some questions; make note of these. Some of these questions will be answered during the class orientation, which could be online or on campus. *If you still have questions, contact the professor and ask him or her.*

6 Review the Textbook

Reviewing the textbook prior to the beginning of a class helps you gain a big-picture understanding of the topics to be covered in the course. By reviewing the table of contents, chapter subtopics, and chapter structure, you create an *advanced organizer* where you store new information. An advanced organizer is similar to shelves in your pantry or cupboards where there is a spot for cereal, canned goods, and baking ingredients. When you review the overall topics and structure of the book, you are creating mental shelves, an advanced organizer, where you organize and store new information. The following are some things to look for when reviewing your textbook and other course materials:

- *Table of contents:* What are the major topics to be covered in this course?
- *Main headings and subheadings:* How are the main topics and subtopics organized in the chapter? How many levels of headings are in the text?
- *Preface:* Does the preface provide you with information on how the text is structured and the special features included in the text?
- *Marginal notes:* Are there marginal notes? If so, what kind of information is included in the marginal notes?
- *Chapter summary:* How is this information structured and how much detail is included?
- *Online review material:* Are there online review materials? If so, which ones would be the most useful to help you review the chapter and prepare for quizzes and tests?
- *End-of-chapter exercises:* What types of end-of-chapter exercises are included in the text? Are these assigned as assignments for the class (check syllabus)?

Don't limit this textbook review to the beginning of the term. It is also a good idea to review each chapter as it is assigned and before reading it to better develop your advanced organizer.

7 Log in to Your Course Learning Management System

As an online student, you will probably use a *learning management system (LMS)* in an online course. An LMS is a secure web site that you log on to. The course LMS has information about the course, assignments, quizzes, tests, forums or bulletin boards, grades, communication options, and various other features. Some of the common LMSs are Blackboard, Canvas, Desire2Learn, Moodle, and Angel.

Usually, the professor for an online course opens the LMS prior to the beginning of the course. It is a good idea to log in to this site early to orient yourself to the structure and content in the LMS. Peruse the different content and pages available. This also creates an advanced organizer for you as you begin the work for this course.

You usually receive an email before the course begins with your log on information, which is typically the user name and password you use to log in to your school web site for registration. If you're not sure about the LMS that you will be using for the course or you don't know how to log in to it, contact (email or phone) your professor and politely ask if the LMS for the course is available.

LEARNING MANAGEMENT SYSTEMS
More information on how to use your LMS more effectively is covered in *Part 4: Learning Management Systems (LMS)* beginning on page 19.

8 Visit Professors' Web Sites

Additionally, your professors might have web sites to provide you with information about their courses. Before the course begins, take time to visit their web sites. You can usually learn a little about your professors and get some general information about the courses you are taking. The following are some items to look for on your professors' web sites:

- Contact information
- Office hours
- Course syllabi
- Textbook and other course material information
- Links to LMS and other important online resources
- General announcements and information

> **PROFESSOR CONTACT INFORMATION**
> Check the school's web site for contact information (email and web site) for your professors. If unable to find this information, call the school.

9 Get to Campus Early

Even though you are taking online courses, there are times you might have to attend an orientation or class on campus. If you have to attend an on-campus meeting, make sure you get there early because *parking tends to be crazy the first couple weeks of class.* If public transportation is an option, consider using it. Many colleges offer students discounts for public transportation.

10 Review the Syllabus before and after the First Class

When taking an online course, the first day of class can be a little ambiguous; it might be an online or on-campus orientation, or it could be an introductory first assignment you complete and turn in. Even though you have already reviewed the syllabus, it is a good idea to review it again after the orientation or first assignment. Reviewing the syllabus helps to clarify your professor's expectations and overall course structure. Also, this helps you ask your professor intelligent and articulate questions to clarify any aspect of this course that might still be confusing. *Don't be afraid to ask your professor questions.*

PART 1: DO SOMETHING ABOUT IT

DISCUSS IT

1.1. What questions should you have asked your academic counselor, which you didn't, when you first met? What are some questions you'll ask at your next meeting?

1.2. After looking over the syllabi for your courses, what are the differences between them? What are the strengths and weaknesses? What makes a good syllabus?

1.3. How did you purchase your textbooks? Did you look at different options? Why did you choose the option you selected?

WRITE IT

1.4. Sometimes we don't know what we don't know until we've had experience with a job, school, course, or personal relationship. Now that you're into your course, write at least three things that you realize you didn't know before you started college. For each of the three items you listed, how did you get your questions answered or where might you find the information you need?

1.5. Do some research and explore at least three support services offered on your campus. Write a summary for each of the three support services detailing the services offered and how you would get these services.

1.6. After attending the orientation for your courses, reviewing the syllabi, text-books, and online resources, make a list of at least five questions you have for your professors.

PART 2: COMMUNICATING WITH YOUR PROFESSORS

Because you do not see your professors face-to-face on a regular basis, it is important to communicate regularly and effectively with them. The tips below will help you to communicate and keep open the lines of communication with your professors, which enhances your success in your courses and decreases your frustration.

11 Save Your Professors' Contact Information

Make sure you know your professors' names, and it is a good idea to store their contact information in both your phone and your computer. *Save their email addresses, phone numbers, and web site addresses* as contacts in your email, on your computer, and on your phone. You never know when you might need to contact them, and you always want to be prepared. It is also a good idea to save the phone number for the school on your phone and computer.

> **TIPS FOR USING EMAIL**
> See *Part 3: Using Email* (beginning on page 12) for a variety of tips for using email effectively.

12 Notify Your Professor Sooner Rather Than Later

As a college student your life is busy with school, work, family, relationships, friends, and various social activities. There will inevitably be emergencies in your life. Be aware that these will happen, and have a plan in place to help you take action when these unexpected situations occur.

As mentioned previously, it is important to have your professors' contact information available on your phone and computer. If for some unexpected reason you are not able to complete assignments, quizzes, or tests by the due date, *contact your professors and let them know before the due date, not after.* Also, be realistic about what constitutes an emergency. If you wait until the last minute to complete an assignment or test and something comes up that night, this is not necessarily an emergency. Expecting the unexpected is another reason for managing your time wisely and working ahead.

13 Be Clear, Concise, and Polite

As a college student, your professors expect you to communicate in a professional and intelligent manner. When emailing or calling a professor, think about the purpose of the communication: What is the specific reason you're calling or emailing him or her?

7

Email

Many of the communication suggestions listed previously also pertain to a written message. Some other considerations for email communication include:

- Use an appropriate email account. Avoid using email addresses such as **hotmama007@gmail.com** or **bigdaddy1991@hotmail.com**.
- Use an appropriate subject line.
- Highlight important information. Consider using bold, underlining, or bulleted or numbered lists.
- Be specific and don't ramble.
- Keep it brief—one or two paragraphs.
- Proofread your message; you want to send a professional, error-free message. Use spell and grammar check.
- Include your name and contact information at the end of the message in the body of the email.
- Proofread again before sending.

> **NUMBERED V. BULLETED LISTS**
> Use numbered lists when the order of the items is important. Use bulleted lists when the order of items is not important.

Phone Call

Prior to your phone call think through the questions you are going to ask and even potential follow-up questions. The following are some ideas to consider before calling a professor:

- Write down a list of questions to ask, which helps you to remember what you need to ask and to keep you focused.
- Clearly state your name and the class in which you are enrolled.
- If leaving a message, speak clearly, leave your phone number, and repeat it at the end of the message.
- Refer specifically to an assignment, page in the book, or item in the syllabus.
- Ask questions; avoid just making statements. Your professors can answer specific questions, but it is difficult to respond to statements.
- Don't ramble. Your professors are there to help you, but be considerate of their time. You want to value and use your time in a productive manner.

Effective communication not only enhances the exchange of information between you and your professors, but also, if you communicate effectively and professionally, your professors will have a better view of your abilities and your desire to be successful in their courses.

14 Use "I" Rather Than "You" When Making Statements

How you speak or write messages largely contributes to how those messages are received. You want to do everything possible to ensure that your messages are received in the manner you intended them to be received.

It is best to use "I" rather than "you" when making statements. "You" statements tend to have a negative connotation and accusatory tone, while "I" statements do not normally carry this negative connotation. For example:

Negative connotation: *"Your instructions on page 4 of the syllabus were vague."*

Better: *"I am having difficulty understanding the instruction #2 on page 4 of the syllabus. Can you clarify this instruction for me?"*

Negative connotation: *"The book is totally unclear about the differences between a positive and persuasive letter."*

Better: *"I am not clear about the differences between a positive and persuasive letter. Will you help me make the distinction between these two types of letters?"*

Negative connotation: *"You marked me wrong on question #5."*

Better: *"On the last quiz, I got question #5 wrong. Will you explain the correct answer?"*

Reserve "you" statements for conveying positive information, and be generous in giving praise to others.

> **"I" STATEMENTS**
> "I" statements also help to improve your communication in personal relationships.

15 Ask for Clarification and Expectations

You will encounter assignments and readings that might not be as clear as you would have wanted. You might not understand what you are expected to do. ***Don't be afraid to ask for clarification.*** Using "I" statements and questions as shown above, politely ask for clarification.

When asking for clarification or expectations, use the following guidelines:

1. *Make an "I" statement:* Clearly and specifically explain what it is you don't understand.

2. *Ask a question:* Follow up with a specific question to which your instructor can respond.

Statement: *"I am not sure what kind of response is needed from me on Forum Post #5."*

Question: *"Does this response need to be formatted as a business letter, or are you just looking for a couple of paragraphs for my response?"*

16 Allow Time to Respond

In this age of smart phones, texting, Facebook, and Twitter, we are conditioned to expect immediate responses from others with whom we communicate. When communicating with your professors, it is professional and courteous to give them time to respond to you. ***Don't expect an immediate response.***

It is standard practice in online courses to give your professors 24–48 hours to respond to your email or phone call. If you email, submit an assignment, or call with a question on Friday afternoon, you should not expect a response until Monday or Tuesday. If you email a professor at 8 p.m. to ask a question about an assignment that is due at midnight, you will probably not, and should not, expect to receive a response. This is good reason to work ahead and not procrastinate. ***Be realistic about the communication expectations you have of your professors.***

> **PROCRASTINATION**
> More information about procrastination is covered *#53: Eliminate Procrastination* on page 30.

17 Schedule Meetings

Sometimes it just not possible to get the help you need via email or a phone call; recognize when this is the case. If you're in a situation where the college campus is close, schedule an appointment with your instructor. The following are some things to keep in mind when meeting with your professors:

- Find out your professors' office hours, and try to schedule meetings during those times.
- If office hours don't work, ask if there are other times available to schedule an appointment. Keep in mind that you might have to change your schedule to make an appointment happen.
- When you set up meetings, inform your professors about the topics you want to discuss; this will help your professors to be prepared and make the most effective use of your time.
- Be prepared for the meeting. Come with a list of specific questions.
- Be on time. Allow for travel time, and find out the location of their offices before you get there.
- Bring your book and any other materials that will be needed.
- Thank your professors for their time.

PART 2: DO SOMETHING ABOUT IT

DISCUSS IT

2.1. Why is it important to notify your instructors sooner rather than later if issues come up during the course? What message do your professors infer from your communication when you contact them before a due date? After a due date?

2.2. How does clarity, conciseness, and politeness contribute to effective communication? What are the effects when communication lacks clarity, conciseness, and politeness?

2.3. Do your professors have policies regarding when you should expect an email response back from them? Are they reasonable? What standard of email response timeliness do you set for yourself? What response expectations do you have from friends, family, and coworkers?

WRITE IT

2.4. Describe the differences between "I" statements and "you" statements and when each should be used. Write three negative "you" statements and three contrasting positive "I" statements.

2.5. Write a message to one of your professors asking for clarification or expectations. Write a clear, concise, and polite message, and use "I" statements as appropriate.

2.6. When scheduling a meeting with a professor, whether it's in person or a phone call, it's important to be prepared. Write a list of things to do to prepare for the meeting, and write at least three specific questions you will ask.

PART 3: USING EMAIL

Most likely you are very comfortable using email and the program/provider you use for email, whether it is Outlook, Gmail, Yahoo, Live, Hotmail, or an email account through your Internet service provider. If you're not, spend some time familiarizing yourself with the available email features. The following suggestions will help you to more effectively and efficiently use email.

18 Check Your Email Regularly

Because you are taking an online or hybrid course, the primary means of communication is email. *Check your email daily.* You are responsible for all information sent to you through email. In your daily schedule, set aside at least one, if not two, times a day to send, read, and respond to email.

19 Manage Email Accounts

MICROSOFT OUTLOOK
Microsoft Outlook is an email program that provides you with email, calendar, contacts, and tasks features. You can manage multiple email accounts with Outlook. Outlook comes with most versions of Microsoft Office. It would be worth your time to learn about Outlook.

Many colleges provide you with a student email account, and school-wide communication is done through this account. Make sure you can log in to this account and are familiar with the features. Each school or professor might have requirements regarding the email account you use; make sure you know what these are.

Many college student email accounts are somewhat antiquated and clunky, lacking many of the features available in Outlook or the free email accounts, such as Gmail, Yahoo, or Live. If you have the choice, *choose one email account to use for all of your school work and correspondence.* This might require that you set up your college student email account to forward to your preferred email account. This can usually be done in the "Settings" or "Preferences." If you choose to use an email account that is not your college account, make sure it is a professional-looking account; don't use provocative, vulgar, or unprofessional words in your email address.

20 Add Email Addresses to Your Contacts/Address Book

Another way to use email effectively and stay organized is to add individuals to your email contacts. All email systems provide you with an area to store contacts. In addition to storing the name and email address of an individual, most email systems will let you to an add address, phone number, and company information. The following are a few ways to add individuals to your contacts:

- Create a new contact and type in the information.

- From an email you receive, you can add the sender's name and email address to your contacts.
- If an individual is in the recipient list of an email you receive, you can add his or her name and email address to your contacts.

Saving and using contacts has a couple distinct advantages. It's quicker to choose a recipient from your contacts. Selecting recipients from contacts is also more accurate than typing an email address; one wrong letter, number, or character and your intended recipient will not receive the email.

> **NETWORKING**
> Classmates and professors are a potential source of professional networking contacts. Record these contacts in the *Contacts* section on page 61.

21 Organize Your Email

Managing email can sometimes be overwhelming. There are some tools that can help you organize and manage your email more effectively.

Folders

Rather than having all of your emails unorganized in your Inbox, you can create folders to store your emails. For example, you can create a folder for each of your courses, one for school-wide information, and one for financial aid. This provides you with a place to move emails. Outlook and most email accounts allow you to create folders.

Rules

Most email programs let you create rules which automatically perform actions on emails when they are received. For example, you can create a rule that would look for the words "Business Communication" or "BUS 310" in the subject line and automatically move that email to the "BUS 310" folder. It is worthwhile to learn how to create and use rules with your email account.

22 Always Use a Subject Line

In every email you send, *use a brief and descriptive subject line.* As you are composing an email message, think about the main topic; make this the subject line of your email. *Don't ever send a message without a subject line.*

Many professors ask for specific information in the subject line. This information will usually be included in the syllabus. For example, students may be asked to put their names, course codes, and assignments (e.g., *Sally Student | 12593 | Text Assign. 1*) in the subject lines of each email they send to a professor. This may allow professors' email rules to automatically move these emails to specific folders, which helps them be more effective and efficient in responding to students.

23 Keep It Brief

When sending email messages to professors or classmates, keep your messages brief; say what needs to be said and don't ramble. A good rule of thumb is if you have to scroll down to read the entire message, it's too long. ***Be clear and specific yet succinct.***

Highlight important information or questions with bold, italic, or underline format. Consider using numbered or bulleted lists for important information.

24 Use a Positive Tone

Try to use a positive tone in all of your email messages. Using a positive tone gives your messages a better chance of coming across as you intended. In communication theory, ***interference*** is what distorts the message so that what is implied by the sender is not what is inferred by the receiver. In oral communication, interference can be body language or delivery style. In written communication, interference is usually caused by message tone or word choice.

If you have to send a negative email message, still try to use as positive of tone as possible. The following are some suggestions for writing negative messages:

- Use passive rather than active verbs and sentence structure. Passive verbs and sentence structure tends to come across as less negative.
- Don't write about feelings. Feelings are very subjective.
- Don't write when you're angry.
- Use "I" rather than "you" statements (see *#14* on page 9).
- Write the message and save it in your *Drafts* folder. Come back to it a day later to see if you can modify it to more clearly and positively convey your message.

25 Use Professional Language and Style

The email messages you send to classmates and professors reflect who you are. You always want to present yourself in the most professional way when corresponding in an educational setting. Use professional and clear language in all of your emails. This does not mean that you have to use big or fancy words. Don't use a fancy-sounding word when a plain and simple word will suffice. ***You want to sound professional, not pretentious.***

Also, be careful about using all capital or lower case letters, decorative fonts, colors, backgrounds, and graphics in your emails. These tend to come across as unprofessional. Limit the use of emoticons and abbreviations you might use when texting a friend. ***Don't write an email message like you would text a friend.***

    Remember . . . once you send an email, it is a public document.

26 Use Proper Grammar and Spelling

Just as using proper tone, language, and style are important to ensure your message is received as intended, the use of proper spelling and grammar is also extremely important. ***The spelling and grammar you use in your email messages reflects your intelligence.***

    Most email systems come equipped with at least a spell check feature, and some also check grammar. Use these features! But don't solely rely on the spelling and grammar checkers to catch all of your mistakes; you must also proofread.

27 Proofread Your Email before Sending

The spelling and grammar checkers available in most email systems catch and help you to correct many errors, but not all of them. These features do not correct improper word choice, all grammar mistakes, poor tone, or unprofessional language and style. It is up to you to proofread your email messages.

    You should always proofread your entire message before sending it. ***Many times your mind reads what you intend to say rather than what you have actually written in the message.*** The following are some tips to help you proofread more effectively:

- Read the message aloud and word for word.
- Look for clear and concise wording in each sentence.
- Look for vague wording and statements.
- Set it aside and come back to it later to proofread again.
- If it is a very important message, have someone else proofread it also.

28 Always Put Your Name at the End of an Email Message

Putting your name below the message in the body of each email is a good habit to get into for a couple of reasons. It is professional to include your name at the conclusion of a message. Also, this adds another layer of protection for the recipient of the message. When a computer becomes infected with a malicious virus, it can hijack your email and send messages to those in your address book. But these viruses don't typically include your name at the bottom of the malicious message. Putting your name in the message helps to protect your reputation and recipients from opening a virus-infected message.

Signatures can be used with most email systems to automatically include your name in the body of all new, reply, and forwarded messages. Each email system is different, so you will have to explore to find out how to do this with the email account you use.

29 Reply to Email

As mentioned previously, it is important to check your email regularly (see *#18* on page 12). It is also important to **reply to emails in a timely manner.** Some emails just need a quick acknowledgement reply such as "Thank you for the research links." or "I received the due date reminder. Thank you." Other emails will require more time and thought to complete.

Always respond quickly to emails asking you a question or to respond with some information. If it is going to take you more than 24 hours to get the answer or information and respond to the email, reply with a short, polite email acknowledging the question or request, and then later follow up with the requested information in another email.

It is also important to know when to end an email conversation. After a couple "Thank you!," "No, thank you," "No. . .no, thank you," it's time to end it and not reply.

30 Use Reply to All, Cc, and Bcc Sparingly

You receive many emails that are addressed to multiple recipients. **Use "Reply to All" only when it is essential that the sender and all original recipients receive your response.** Most of the time a response to the sender only (*Reply*) is all that is needed. The exception to this rule is when working on a group project. It is important to keep all members of your group in the loop with important information about the project on which you are working. **Use good judgment when deciding whether to use "Reply" or "Reply to All."**

Cc and *Bcc* are two other email addressing options. **Cc stands for copy** and **Bcc is a blind copy.** If there is an important or tense email discussion occurring when working on a group project, it is a good idea to copy (Cc) your professor so he or she is kept informed about the interactions within the group. When recipients are placed in the *Bcc* line, the other recipients do not see the names and email addresses of those in the *Bcc* line. A blind copy is commonly used when sending an email to a group of recipients and confidentiality of the recipients is required or desired.

When recipients are in the *Cc* or *Bcc* line, they will receive the message just as the other recipients, and they are able to reply or forward without restrictions.

31 Conquer Your Email Inbox

For most of us, the volume of emails received each day can be overwhelming. The following are some tips to help you control your email *Inbox,* rather than letting it control you:

Read: Select a couple chunks of time throughout your day to dedicate to reading your emails. After reading each email, take action on it. The content and context of the message will determine what to do with it: ***reply, reorganize,*** and/or ***remove.***

Reply: Not all emails need a response, but to those that do, try to respond to as quickly as possible. This will not only make you more responsive to others, but also complete a task that will most likely have to be done at some point in the future.

Reorganize: Decide whether or not a message needs to be kept and then use one or more of the following email features to keep your email organized: *Follow Up Flags, Categories, Rules,* or *Folders.* You can also create a calendar item, task, or note from the content of an email.

Remove: Delete email messages that are no longer needed. Messages to which you have previously replied are stored in your *Sent Items* folder. You can always search this folder if, by chance, you need a particular message in the future, which you probably won't.

- ***Unsubscribe:*** Most of us receive numerous advertisement emails daily. Usually, there is a link at the bottom of these messages to remove yourself from the mailing list.

- ***Conversation Clean Up:*** Using the conversation clean up tools will delete redundant email messages in the threaded conversation.

- ***Empty Deleted Items:*** Set up your email account so it automatically deletes all items in your *Deleted Items* folder each time you exit (if you're using Outlook) or periodically empty this folder.

PART 3: DO SOMETHING ABOUT IT

DISCUSS IT

3.1.   Which of your email accounts is your favorite and why? Why is it important to use one email account for all of your college communication? Why is it important to check your email?

3.2.   Do you proofread most of your emails before you send them? Why is it important to proofread emails before sending? Does it make a difference to whom you're sending the email?

3.3.   Why is it important to include an appropriate subject line and your name in the body of the message on each email you send? Do you use signatures? What are other uses of signatures?

WRITE IT

3.4.   Write a brief message to one of your professors to set up a meeting. Use an appropriate subject line, keep the body of the message brief and specific, use a positive tone and professional language, and proofread carefully.

3.5.   Write at least three benefits of organizing your emails using folders and rules, and write a list of folders you will need for your courses this term. Think carefully through your folder structure. Do you need folders for group projects, financial aid, or student support services?

3.6.   Explain the difference between *Reply* and *Reply All* and when is it appropriate to use each. Explain the difference between *Cc* and *Bcc* and when you might use each.

PART 4: LEARNING MANAGEMENT SYSTEMS (LMS)

Learning management systems (LMS) are ubiquitous in online education. There are many LMSs on the market, and they vary in their structure and capabilities. But there are many commonalities among the different LMSs. This section explains some of these common features and provides suggestions to help you use your LMS to enhance your learning.

LMS V. CMS
A learning management system (LMS) can also be referred to as a content management system (CMS).

32 Get to Know Your LMS

An LMS can be used in your online courses for distributing information, completing assignments, taking quizzes and tests, posting responses to a discussion board or forum, posting grades, communicating with students and professors, and other features. Some of the more common LMSs are listed below:

- Blackboard
- Canvas
- Moodle
- Desire2Learn
- Angel

As mentioned earlier, it will be helpful to log in to your course LMS before the course begins. Peruse the LMS to familiarize yourself with the layout and content. It is also helpful to have your syllabus available while browsing around your LMS to recognize how they relate to each other. The following are some questions to ask yourself as you navigate through your LMS:

- What information is available?
- Is there a calendar or schedule listing assignment due dates?
- What course activities will be completed in the LMS?
- Is there an email/communication feature? If so, does it connect to your email?
- How do I view my grades? Are these my overall grades?
- How can I change my password and update my profile?
- How can I retrieve my password if I forget it?

LMS TUTORIAL
Most LMSs have a tutorial or help feature built in, which helps you to understand the structure and components of your LMS.

If you take the time to familiarize yourself with the LMS before the term begins, it is easier to ask a professor specific questions regarding the LMS as the need arises.

33 Select the Proper Internet Browser

Both Internet browsers and LMSs are regularly updated and continually improved, but there are certain browsers that might work better with your LMS. This information can usually be found in your syllabus or on the log on page for your LMS. Some of the most common Internet browsers are:

- Mozilla Firefox
- Google Chrome
- Internet Explorer

It is important to use the most current versions of your browsers. Internet browsers are free, and you are normally prompted to upload the most current version when a new version of your browser is released. You can find out if your browser is up to date by navigating to the *About* menu.

Figure 1 Browser version information

34 Security Settings: Pop-Up Windows

Internet browsers work diligently at blocking unwanted pop-up windows. You might run into the issue of your LMS being blocked as a pop-up window by your browser. If this is the case, you can create an exception to allow the URL (web address) of your LMS and not block it as a pop-up window. To do this, go into the options and locate the "block pop-ups" menu; this varies depending on your browser. You can add your LMS web address to allow as an exception.

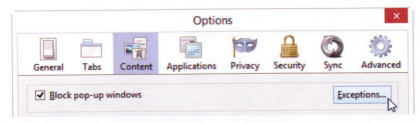

Figure 2 Add exceptions to your browser's pop-up blocker

35 Update Preferences

In your LMS, there is probably a *Preferences* or *Option* area where you can customize your personal information. You might be able to change your password or email address or add a picture and a brief personal description. Sometimes you can change the color of the LMS environment and how you receive forum or discussion board posts. Browse through these preference options after familiarizing yourself with the LMS.

36 Use FAQs

FAQs or "frequently asked questions" is a common area in most LMSs. FAQs list common questions and responses to those questions. There might be two different sets of FAQs in your LMS. One might cover general questions and answers about your LMS. The other might be FAQs pertaining to your course. Most likely if you have a question about your course, others have previously asked the same question. **Browse through the FAQs about your course and familiarize yourself with the common questions.** If you are familiar with the common questions, you are able to quickly find an answer as a question arises.

> **QUESTIONS**
> Some instructors set up a *Questions* area so students can ask questions and receive responses from other students or professors. Scan through these regularly to see if you can answer a question for a classmate.

37 Explore Other Online Learning Resources

In addition to your course LMS, many textbooks come with online learning resources. You might have to complete assignments on these online learning environments. Online learning resources that are associated with your textbooks provide you with excellent review and study material such as practice quizzes, review activities, PowerPoint slides outlining chapters, supplementary readings, or enrichment projects.

Some of these online resources might be connected to your LMS, but many are not and require a different user name and password to log in to the system. If you are using one or more of these online resources, *take the time to log in to these online systems and familiarize yourself with content available.*

38 Know Due Dates

In an online course, it is your responsibility to keep up with the assigned work for the course. Due dates for discussion board and forum posts, assignments, quizzes, tests, and projects are usually listed in the syllabus, and they are, many times, also listed in the LMS. *Log into your LMS regularly to check for upcoming assigned work.* Use the LMS and syllabus in conjunction to make sure you are completing all assigned work by the due date. If you use a calendar in your email system, phone, or an organizer, enter the due dates to help keep you organized.

39 Post and Respond to Discussion Boards and Forums

Discussion boards and forums are used in online courses to facilitate discussions about various course topics. These discussions are used in lieu of class discussions that occur in a traditional classroom environment. Each professor uses discussion boards differently. Become familiar with the different types of discussions you will be using in your courses.

Sometimes a discussion board or forum post requires you to respond to a specific topic, question, or writing prompt. Other times you also respond to the responses of others. The following are a few tips for responding to discussion boards:

> **WRITING ASSIGNMENTS**
> More detailed information about writing assignments is available in *Part 7: Writing Assignments* beginning on page 35.

- Read the topic, question, or writing prompt carefully.
- Make sure you know the information pertaining to the topic. Complete the chapter readings before responding to a discussion board topic.
- Be specific and succinct.
- Use a positive and respectful tone when responding to others' posts.

40 Work Ahead

In your courses, *it is much easier and less stressful to stay caught up on your class assignments than it is to catch up.* Plan ahead and do as much work as possible before the due dates. This includes reading the assigned chapters in your textbooks, reviewing PowerPoint slides and lecture notes, completing writing assignments, and making discussion board posts. One tremendous advantage of working ahead is the option of asking your professors questions and having time for them to respond before the due dates.

PART 4: DO SOMETHING ABOUT IT

DISCUSS IT

4.1. Which LMS are you using for your classes? Have you used other LMSs in the past for other courses, and if so, how do they compare with your current LMS? Are there other online learning resources associated with your courses or textbooks? If so, what is the quality of these online resources?

4.2. What are the advantages of working ahead? How does this influence the quality of your work? How does knowing and keeping track of due dates help you work ahead?

4.3. Do you like responding to discussion boards or forums, and why or why not? What is the most challenging aspect to these writings? What are you learning from these writings?

WRITE IT

4.4. Discussion board or forum writings can be challenging, especially if your peers are responding to your writings. Write a paragraph describing the strategies you'll use when writing these and responding to your classmates' writings. Write another paragraph describing how you will use feedback from your instructor and classmates to improve your thinking and writing.

4.5. Make a list of at least three strengths and three weaknesses of your LMS. Write a brief paragraph of how you would make your LMS more user friendly.

4.6. Make a list of upcoming assignments, projects, quizzes, and tests in all of your classes for the next two weeks. List the dates each is available, due dates of each, and the dates you will begin working on each.

PART 5: MANAGING TIME AND STAYING ORGANIZED

One of the most important things you can do to ensure your success in online courses is to stay organized. It is up to you to do those things that will help you stay organized.

41 Set a Schedule and Stick to It

As you begin your online courses, it is important for you to create a schedule and stick to it. Just as you would if you were taking an onsite course, schedule hours throughout the week to work on your course work. *Be very specific; set certain days and times to do your work on a specific course, and do this for each of your courses.* The weekly schedule grid, inside the front cover of this book, is a tool you can use to create your schedule. Use a pencil so adjustments can be made if needed.

Be realistic about time requirements for courses, work, and family and personal life. When filling out your weekly schedule, make sure you not only include your classes, but also include work and family and personal time. The following are some other suggestions and general guidelines to help you create your weekly schedule:

- For a three-unit course, schedule six hours a week.
- Schedule time in 1.5- or 2-hour chunks, 3 to 4 days a week.
- Don't try to do all of your work for a class in one day.
- Schedule family, personal, and recreational time.
- Leave some "wiggle room" in your schedule. Sometimes homework might take longer than expected, or the unexpected and unplanned event might occur (remember Murphy's Law).
- Leave room in your schedule for at least 7 hours of sleep each night.

There is always an episode of *The Voice, The Big Bang Theory,* or *CSI* on TV for you to watch, and Facebook, Twitter, and video games can be enticing. Creating a realistic schedule helps you eliminate the "I'll get to my homework sometime" attitude.

42 Use the Syllabus and LMS

As mentioned previously, the syllabus and LMS are extremely important; they are your road maps to success in each course. It's not only important to review the syllabus and peruse the LMS before the course begins, but also regularly (daily) throughout the term—embrace the syllabus and LMS. The following are some of the items to look for as you review the syllabus and LMS regularly:

- Due dates
- Assignments that can be completed early
- Feedback on assignments
- Grades
- Links to supplementary online resources
- Supplemental readings

43 Use a Planner for Due Dates and Other Information

Since you are using this book, you are already on the right track in staying organized. Using a planner such as this book, and electronic planners (email system and smart phone) will help you to stay organized. *But it requires more than just having these resources; you must also regularly use them.* The following are some of the items you want to keep in your planner:

- Weekly schedule (inside front cover)
- Due dates for assignments, quizzes, and tests
- Project due dates
- Appointments with professors or counselors
- Dates of online or on-site workshops
- Additional course notes (page 88)
- Online resources (page 54)
- Group members' contact information (page 61)
- Professors' contact information (page 64)
- Professional and networking contacts' information (page 67)

44 Plan for the Unexpected

Expecting the unexpected is another way to help you stay organized. No matter how structured and organized you are, there are always unforeseen circumstances that occur in your life, some of which you have little or no control over. *By being organized and prepared in advance, you will have more time and options available to you when these situations occur.*

The next section, *Enhancing Study Skills,* will give you more specific suggestions about how to better manage your time.

45 Check Grades Regularly

Checking your grades regularly (at least weekly) is an excellent way to help you stay organized. Not only does checking your grades keep you updated on your progress in the course, but it also alerts you to missing assignments and upcoming assignments, quizzes, and tests.

Knowing your grades and reviewing your graded assignments also contributes to increased motivation (see *Part 10: Staying Motivated throughout the Course* beginning on page 51) and improved study skills (see *Part 6: Enhancing Study Skills* beginning on page 29).

46 Bookmark Important Online Resources

Whichever Internet browser you use, you have the ability to add a **Bookmark** or add to **Favorites** your frequently used and important web sites. This feature allows you to store this information on your computer so you can easily and quickly get to these web sites. This saves you the time of either typing in the URL or using a search engine to locate the web site. If you use multiple computers, consider storing the bookmarks on each computer. Some of the web sites you should bookmark are:

- Course LMS
- Professors' web sites
- College web site and some of the specific pages within that site (e.g., course schedule, term calendars, course catalog, and enrollment services)
- Online learning center or student resource web sites associated with your textbooks
- FAFSA web site
- Other online learning resources (see *Part 11: Using Online Resources* page 54)

47 Use a High-Quality Computer and Internet Connection

Having an up-to-date computer and high-speed Internet connection are essential when taking online courses. Most of your work for online courses will be completed using your computer and various web sites, so having a quality computer and fast and stable Internet connection helps you avoid unnecessary delays and frustration.

If you are buying a new computer, *you don't need to buy a top-of-the-line computer to have a high-quality computer.* You can purchase a good computer that will last you four to five years for a reasonable price. Before purchasing a computer, make sure you do some research about processor speed, memory, storage, screen size, laptop versus desktop, and any other features that interest you. Once you've done your research and know what you are looking for in a computer, there are two different strategies to use when purchasing a computer.

- Determine the amount of money you want to spend and then search for the best computer and features for that price.
- List the specific features you want in the computer (e.g., processor speed, memory, storage, and monitor), and find the best price for a computer equipped with these features.

48 Choose the Correct Software

The type of courses you are taking in college will, to some extent, determine the types of software you will need on your computer. Always check your syllabi for specific software requirements. Some of the essentials are:

- Internet browser
- Word processor
- Presentation software

Other types of programs could include:

- Email program
- Spreadsheet
- Database
- Graphics software
- Video editing

There are both paid and free versions of software available. Microsoft Office, Office 365, and Adobe are some of the leading software for both business and education. *Most colleges have educational discounts available on these programs, and there are some web sites that offer education discounts to college students.* Google Docs, Office Web Apps, and OpenOffice are free software products that include a word processor, spreadsheet, database, and presentation software.

> **DISCOUNT AND FREE SOFTWARE**
> See *Part 11: Using Online Resources* (beginning on page 54) for more information on educational discounts and free software.

49 Update Computer Skills

Your computer and accompanying software are magnificent tools to help you in your personal, educational, and professional life. If you are a computer novice, you might consider taking a computer course before, or in conjunction with, your online course. *It is important to know the basics of the operating systems, file management, and word processing.* In the long run, you will save time and be less frustrated if you have some of these basic computer skills.

There are many free online training resources available (see *Part 11: Using Online Resources* page 54). If you are lacking some of these basic computer skills, take advantage of these free online resources.

PART 5: DO SOMETHING ABOUT IT

DISCUSS IT

5.1.   What type of unexpected events tend to mess up your schedule? What do you do to plan for the unexpected?

5.2.   How would you rate your computer skills? What type of computer classes have you had in the past? What are your strong computer skills? In what areas do you need to improve your computer skills?

5.3.   Do you currently use a schedule? Why or why not? If you use a schedule, how has this helped you manage your time and stay organized? How often should you update your schedule?

WRITE IT

5.4.   Create a schedule for this term. Use *#41: Set a Schedule and Stick to It* as a guide. Be sure to include your courses, work, study time, personal time, and other as needed.

5.5.   Make a list of at least 10 web sites to bookmark in your Internet browser.

5.6.   Use the calendar in this book (beginning on page 61) to record due dates of assignments, projects, quizzes, and tests for the next month. Write a brief paragraph describing how you plan for unexpected events.

PART 6: ENHANCING STUDY SKILLS

When taking a traditional on-campus course, much of the organization and time management is built into the structure of attending class on certain days at a specific time. But you're taking an online course, and it is up to you to manage your time wisely. This section will provide you with suggestions to manage your time and improve your study skills.

50 Know Your Learning Style

Your learning style is reflected in how you prefer to acquire, process, and retain new information. There are four main categories of learning styles:

- *Visual:* This individual prefers learning from diagrams, charts, pictures, videos, and concept maps.
- *Auditory:* This individual prefers learning from spoken words and may find note taking distracting.
- *Read/Write:* This individual prefers learning from a written format such as a book or notes.
- *Kinesthetic:* This individual prefers learning by doing hands-on activities.

Can you determine your preferred learning style?

VARK LEARNING STYLES

For more information about VARK learning styles and an online assessment, see page 56 or visit the following web site: http://www.vark-learn.com.

51 Know Your Personality Type

There are many different personality scales and tests. One of the most common and reputable is the *Myers-Briggs Type Indicator.* Myers-Briggs classifies personality types into four main categories and places individuals into one of two groups in each of these categories, which creates the following 16 possible personality types:

- *Favorite World:* **Extrovert (E) or Introvert (I)**

  Do you prefer to focus on the outer world or on your own inner world?
- *Information*: **Sensing (S) or Intuition (N)**

  Do you prefer to focus on the basic information you take in or to interpret and add meaning?
- *Decisions*: **Thinking (T) or Feeling (F)**

  When making decisions, do you prefer to first look at logic and consistency, or first look at the people and special circumstances?
- *Structure*: **Judging (J) or Perceiving (P)**

  When dealing with the outside world, do you prefer to get things decided or to stay open to new information and options?

Each group within each category has a letter assigned to it (e.g., INTJ). Can you determine what your personality type is? For more information about the *Myers-Briggs Type Indicator,* visit the following web site: **http://www.myersbriggs.org/**.

52 How Learning Style and Personality Type Affect Your Education

It is very helpful to know your preferred learning style and your personality type. This information can help you better understand yourself, work within your areas of strength, and recognize areas of weakness. Also, understanding your own and knowing the different learning styles and personality types helps you understand and appreciate differences in others, which is extremely important.

The following are some important things to know and think about regarding learning styles and personality types:

- Within each of these learning styles and personality types, there is much individual variance.
- Just because you have a preferred learning style does not imply that you don't have strengths in the other areas.
- Your learning style and personality type might change over the course of your life.
- You can improve in learning styles outside of your preferred learning style.
- Don't use your learning style or personality type as a crutch or excuse.
- Work within your areas of strength, but also work to strengthen other learning and personality styles.
- Use your knowledge of learning styles and personality types to appreciate the differences in others.

53 Eliminate Procrastination

Procrastination is one of largest stumbling blocks of time management and successful learning. ***You need to ruthlessly eliminate procrastination from your lifestyle.*** Procrastination limits your success not only in education but also in your professional and personal life.

Identifying potential time wasters is the first step in eliminating procrastination. Computer games and TV are huge time wasters; you can lose hours without realizing it. Both of these can be great ways to unwind and relax, but carefully monitor yourself when participating in these activities.

The best way to eliminate procrastination is to create a schedule and stick to it (see #41: *Set a Schedule and Stick to It*). Make sure you schedule some personal time. It's unrealistic to have no "down time" built into your schedule.

54 Have a Consistent and Quiet Workplace

Find a specific place that is quiet and free from distractions to do your coursework. Ideally, this would be in your home or apartment. If this is not possible, you might be able to find a quiet room at work, a college or public library, or possibly a friend's home or apartment. It is difficult and disruptive to your schedule if you are always hunting for a place to study. Also, try to find a place that is free from distractors such as TV or video games.

55 Personalize Your Work Space

Another way to make your study time more enjoyable and productive is to create a work space that is organized and personalized. The following are some suggestions:

- Use a desk.
- Get a comfortable chair.
- Stock your desk with pens, pencils, highlighters, paper, index cards, sticky notes, and other school supplies you might need.
- Personalize your work area with pictures and music.
- Keep healthy snacks and a water bottle available.

56 Set Study Goals

As you begin each study session, think about what you plan to accomplish. Much of this is determined by due dates of assignments, quizzes, and tests. Within the overall tasks that must be accomplished, break down how your time will be spent on each task. Set specific study goals. *Take a couple of minutes to write down your study goals before you begin studying.* See the example below:

9:00-9:45	Read Chapter 3
9:45-9:55	Break
9:55-10:20	Discussion board post
10:20-10:30	Break
10:30-11:00	Chapter 3 quiz

Setting study goals helps to keep you focused and productive.

57 Take Frequent Short Breaks

As shown in the study goal schedule above, it is important to schedule and take frequent, short breaks. These breaks refresh you and give your tired brain a needed break. *These breaks are not a waste of time, but rather they make you more productive and focused while you are studying.* The following are some suggestions when taking a break:

- Get up and stretch.
- Walk around.
- Go outside and get some fresh air.
- Get something to eat or drink.
- Check email or text friends.
- Make a phone call.

Doing one or more of these takes your mind off your homework and re-energizes you so you can get back to studying and finish up your tasks.

58 Pre-Read Material

Before you read a chapter in a textbook or lecture notes, *take time to skim through the material looking for main topics and subtopics.* Pay attention to the different levels of headings in the chapter and the text that is bold and italic in the paragraphs. After skimming through the chapter, read the summary at the end of the chapter. Doing this creates an advanced organizer (mental shelves) where you can organize and store new information, ideas, and concepts (see #6: *Review the Textbook* page 3).

59 Take Notes

When reading a chapter in a textbook, lecture notes, or PowerPoint slides, take notes on the material you are reading. By taking notes, you are adding another modality *(writing)* to complement the *reading* modality. This helps you to better retain and recall the information.

Notes can be taken in a variety of formats; you can use an outline, index cards, or a concept map. You need to determine the most effective note-taking method for you. The following are some suggestions to make your note taking more beneficial:

- Think about *meta-concepts;* these are the major ideas or themes in a chapter.
- Use the main headings and subheadings from the chapter in your notes.
- Use short phrases and key words rather than long sentences.

- Leave room on the paper or index card for additional information you might add later.
- Review your notes a day or two later. Reviewing material numerous times over an extended period of time improves retention and recall.

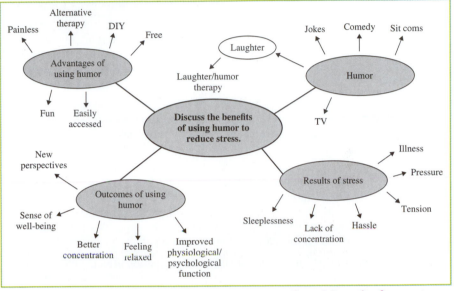

Figure 3 Example of concept map

60 Review Past Assignments

It is important to go back and review graded assignments and tests. On written assignments, the comments given by your professor help you better understand the material. If you are on the right track, these comments will confirm your understanding and application of the material. If there are responses that were incorrect or in need of improvement, these comments help you better comprehend the subject matter. The same applies when reviewing quizzes and tests. If you have something that is incorrect on a written assignment or test, you want to learn why it is incorrect. *Knowing why something is incorrect or how it can be improved is true learning.*

PART 6: DO SOMETHING ABOUT IT

DISCUSS IT

6.1. Describe where you do most of your homework and studying. How does having a consistent and quiet study area enhance your studying? How do you personalize your work space?

6.2. How does your learning style influence how you study for your courses? Are your courses structured more for *visual, auditory, read/write,* or *kinesthetic* learners? Do you think your learning style can change over time? How can you strengthen learning styles that do not come naturally to you?

6.3. Describe how you set study goals. How do study goals help keep you focused during studying? Do you typically pre-read material? Why or why not? How does reviewing past assignments contribute to your learning?

WRITE IT

6.4. Use the Internet to look up information about VARK learning styles and the Myers-Briggs Type Indicator (see links in *#50: Know Your Learning Style* and *#51: Know Your Personality Type* on page 29). Using this information, determine your learning style and your personality type. Write a paragraph describing how this information affects your education.

6.5. Write a brief paragraph describing how procrastination affects your learning and success in your courses. Write a list of at least five effective techniques you can use to eliminate procrastination.

6.6. Select a chapter from one of your textbooks and pre-read the chapter paying attention to headings and heading structure. Read the chapter. Using information from *#59: Take Notes,* create a detailed concept map for the chapter.

PART 7: WRITING ASSIGNMENTS

Teachers often say, "If you want to be a better reader, read. If you want to become a better writer, read. And if you want to become a better thinker, write." Your writing is a reflection of your ability to think. Employers want employees who clearly articulate ideas both orally and in written format. Most of us communicate better orally than in writing. This section gives you some suggestions on ways to improve the quality of your writing.

61 Do Your Very Best Work on Your First Writing Assignment

Your professor forms a first and lasting impression of you based on your first writing assignment. Even though this sounds harsh, it is true. You want to make a great first impression with the quality of your writing. This is especially important in an online environment where you may never meet your professor face to face. The topics in this section provide you specific techniques to improve the quality of your written assignments that will help you make good first and lasting impressions on your professors.

62 Use Writing Resources at Your College and Online

Your professors might provide you with writing style guides that give you information and examples of their writing expectations. Additionally, your college might have a writing center that can provide you with a writing style guide, handouts on MLA and APA report writing and formatting, or writing workshops.

There are also many online resources to help you with writing, formatting reports, and creating accurate citations and references. *One of the best online writing resources is Purdue University's OWL* (Online Writing Lab: **http://owl .english.purdue.edu/owl/**). This web site is very user-friendly and has excellent writing resources for general writing, research and report writing, subject-specific writing, and job search writing.

REPORT WRITING
MLA (Modern Language Association) and APA (American Psychological Association) are two of the most common types of report formats used in college writing.

63 Don't Plagiarize

When writing, it is very important to give credit to your sources. This includes not only material that is directly quoted but also summarized and paraphrased information. *If you take information from other sources and do not give credit to the source of the information, this is plagiarism.* The following list describes how you can effectively use information from other sources:

- *Quote:* Identical to the original source and written within quotation marks; can be a short phrase up to a couple of sentences.
- *Paraphrase:* Idea taken from another source but written in your own words; usually slightly shorter than the original source.
- *Summarize:* Ideas taken from another source but condensed substantially and written in your own words; summarizing typically highlights the main points without going into too much detail.

When quoting, paraphrasing, or summarizing information from other sources, you must provide the source of the information you used in your writing. This is typically done by using a citation in the body of the report and providing full bibliographic information at the end of the report.

- *Citation:* Brief information about the source, such as the author's last name and date of publication; typically included in parentheses after the quoted, paraphrased, or summarized information.
- *Reference:* Full bibliographic information for a source; typically includes author, date, title, and source of publication; usually included at the end of a report on a separate page titled *Works Cited* or *References.*

The format of citations and references will vary depending on whether you are using APA, MLA, or other type of report format. Use handouts from your professor and online resources to help you format citations and references.

To avoid plagiarism, there are two main objectives when using other sources in your writing:

1. Give credit (citations) to ideas and information from others, even paraphrased and summarized information.

2. Provide full bibliographic information (references) for the source of this information.

64 Respond Directly to the Question

A writing assignment is usually a response to a question or scenario. Before you begin to write, make sure you read the question or scenario carefully. Before you begin writing, ask yourself the following questions:

- What is the question or scenario, and do I understand it?
- What is my professor asking of me?
- What type of response is he or she looking for?
- Are there special instructions for this assignment?

As you begin writing, make sure you are responding directly to the question or scenario. It is very easy to go off on a tangent and veer away from the main point of the writing assignment. *Two or three times throughout your writing assignment refer back to the original question or scenario and evaluate whether or not you are still responding directly to it.* Do this again when you finish your assignment.

When you write an essay or long report, you are responding to a specific topic or research question. The same principles listed above also apply to essays, short reports, and research reports.

65 Know and Apply the Chapter Content to Your Writing

In most writing assignments and reports, professors want you to apply, in writing, new information you have learned. Learning has occurred when you can take new information and apply it in a different context. When working on a writing assignment, you not only want to respond directly to the question or scenario but also apply and incorporate the information (e.g., from a textbook, lecture notes, or readings) into your written assignment.

Before you begin writing, ask yourself, "How does the new information I am learning relate to the question or scenario to which I am responding?" The following are some tips to help you apply the chapter content to your writing:

- Read and review the chapter (or required readings) before doing the writing assignment.
- Review your notes (see #59: *Take Notes*).
- Am I including the meta-concept in my writing?
- Am I including relevant and specific details to support the main concepts?

66 Use an Introductory Sentence, Supporting Statements, and a Concluding Sentence

Each writing assignment varies, but normally each paragraph includes an introductory sentence, supporting statements, and a concluding or transition sentence. The *introductory sentence* introduces the topic about which you are writing. *Supporting statements* are used to provide specific details about the topic. It is best to use two to five supporting statements in each paragraph. The *concluding sentence* wraps up the topic about which you are writing. Don't present new information in the conclusion, but rather summarize and present a "So what?" about the paragraph. A *transitional sentence* can be used instead of a concluding sentence as a transition and link to a new paragraph and topic.

67 Vary Sentence Structure

Using a variety of sentence types makes your writing sound more intelligent, improves readability, and makes your writing more interesting. The different types of sentence structures are:

HELP WITH WRITING MECHANICS

The Online Writing Lab (OWL) from Purdue University is an excellent source of information to help you with grammar and sentence structure. See *#97: Learning Resources* on page 54 for more information about OWL.

- *Simple sentence:* One independent clause
- *Compound sentence:* Two independent clauses connected with a conjunction or semi-colon
- *Complex sentence:* An independent clause and one or more dependent clauses
- *Compound-complex sentence:* Two independent clauses and one or more dependent clauses

Knowing the different types of sentence structures helps you analyze your writing. You don't have to use each type of sentence in every paragraph, but examine your writing to ensure that you are using a variety of these four types of sentence structures.

68 Keep Paragraphs Focused

Whether writing a short written assignment or a long research report, it is important to keep your paragraphs focused. *Each paragraph should contain one main point.* As mentioned previously, each paragraph should have an introductory sentence, supporting statements (two to five), and a concluding or transition sentence.

Shorter paragraphs (three to seven sentences) are easier to read and more focused. Long rambling paragraphs tend to lose the main topic of the paragraph. *Each sentence in a paragraph should be related to or support the main topic of the paragraph.* Also, shorter paragraphs are easier to write; each paragraph allows you to concentrate your writing on one main topic.

69 Don't Ramble

Often in students' writing assignments, the writing tends to ramble and go nowhere in particular. It lacks clarity, content, and focus. Some examples of rambling include:

- Not staying focused on the topic.
- Making vague references.
- Using unclear pronoun references.
- Saying the same thing over and over.
- Writing paragraphs without a specific topic.

To help focus your writing and avoid rambling, apply the principles covered above in *#64–#68:*

- Respond directly to the question.
- Know and apply the chapter (or research) content to your writing.

- Use an introductory sentence, supporting statements, and a concluding (or transitional) sentence.
- Vary sentence structure.
- Keep paragraphs focused.

70 Edit and Proofread

The importance of editing and proofreading cannot be over-emphasized. ***Editing and proofreading is not a one-time activity; it is an ongoing process.*** As you are writing your assignment, essay, or report, it is important to proofread along the way; this is primarily for spelling and grammar, and you can make use of the spelling and grammar checkers in the word processing software. Proofreading and editing is not limited to just catching and fixing grammatical and mechanical errors. You also edit the content to ensure that your writing is focused and on topic.

When you finish a writing assignment, allow yourself plenty of time to proofread and edit the document. If you are working on a long essay or report, do this a couple of times throughout the writing process. The following are some tips to make your proofreading and editing more effective:

- ***Content:*** Does your writing directly respond to the topic, writing prompt, or question?
- ***Information:*** Are you applying information and concepts you have learned to the writing assignment?
- ***Clarity:*** Are ideas presented in a clear, specific, and related way? Watch for vague references.
- ***Structure:*** Are you using a variety of sentence structures? Are you using shorter, focused paragraphs? Does each sentence in a paragraph relate to the main topic of that paragraph? Did you include an introductory sentence, supporting sentences, and a concluding (or transitional) sentence?
- ***Format:*** Is your assignment formatted correctly? Read the assignment instructions for specifics on format. Is your assignment consistently formatted throughout the document?

PEER EDITING
You might consider having a classmate, friend, or family member edit and proofread your document and provide feedback. Another set of eyes evaluating your writing will enhance it.

PART 7: DO SOMETHING ABOUT IT

DISCUSS IT

7.1. In past classes, did you do your best work on your first writing assignment? Why or why not? Why is it important to do your best writing at the beginning of the course?

7.2. When do you have to cite a source from which you obtained information for your report or writing? What is the difference between a citation and a reference? What is most challenging about citing sources and creating references?

7.3. What does it mean to "keep paragraphs focused" and why is this important? How does varying sentence structures improve the readability of a paragraph? How do you keep from rambling in your writing?

WRITE IT

7.4. Using your own words, paraphrase *#63: Don't Plagiarize* in one paragraph. In another paragraph, summarize *#64–#70,* to describe how to improve your writing.

7.5. Using your best writing, write a paragraph introducing yourself, describing your past educational experience, and explaining your educational goals. Use *#64–#70* to help you write effectively.

7.6. Use resources from your professor, college, or online to learn how to properly cite a quotation and create a reference in either APA or MLA format. Quote a sentence from this book. Create a citation and a reference for this source in proper APA or MLA format.

PART 8: TAKING TESTS AND QUIZZES ONLINE

Taking tests is not only a part of your education but also a part of your personal and professional life (e.g., driver's license renewal tests, employment tests, recertification exams, and professional development exams). Tests are used to evaluated knowledge and learning. Knowing and using some test-taking strategies can help you improve your performance on tests.

*In this section, the word **"test"** will be used generically to encompass quizzes, tests, and exams, even though there is much variance within these different evaluation instruments.*

71 Know What Type of Test You're Taking

Before taking your test, know whether it is a quiz, test, or exam. Each of these testing instruments has different point values or weight on your overall course grade. Tests and exams are usually worth more points or weighted more heavily on your overall grade, while quizzes are usually worth fewer points. Knowing the importance of a quiz, test, or exam will help you to prepare.

Also, know what material is going to be covered on the test. A quiz might only cover one chapter of material, while a test or exam might cover multiple chapters.

72 Reduce Anxiety

Anxiety and testing seem to go hand in hand, but you can reduce or eliminate testing anxiety. *The more prepared you are for a test, the more confident and relaxed you will be.* Also, it is important to go into the test with a positive attitude. As mentioned previously, a test is a positive opportunity for you to demonstrate your preparedness and knowledge of subject matter you are learning in a course. *A test does not reflect who you are or your self-worth; a test measures knowledge of subject matter.*

Some of the specific things you can do to reduce test anxiety include:

- Get a good night's sleep before the test.
- If you've been studying a while before the test, go outside, take a walk, and get some fresh air.
- Have a snack and some water or juice.
- View the test positively. Reflect on past tests you've "aced."

73 Know and Review the Material

When taking a test, there is no substitute for preparation. *Your performance on a test is directly related to the preparation you have done before taking the test.* Your ability to retain and recall information is improved by studying and reviewing material multiple times over an extended period of time, rather than "cramming" for a test. Some of the specific things you can do before a test to help you prepare are:

- Review the chapter(s) to be covered on the test.
- Review lecture notes and PowerPoint slides.
- Review your notes.
- Review the main and subtopics covered in the chapter(s).
- Review the chapter summary, key words, and concepts.

74 Review Previous Quizzes and Assignments

Part of your preparation for a test should be to review previous material related to the test. If taking a test or exam that covers multiple chapters, review quizzes and assignments related to the test or exam. As you review previous assignments, re-read the questions and your responses. Read your instructor's comments. When reviewing previous quizzes, re-read questions and your answers. If you had an incorrect answer or response on an assignment or quiz, know why it is incorrect; this helps you not make the same mistake again.

If you're in close proximity to the college campus and in contact with other students, consider gathering together for a *study group.* Collectively, the group can review past assignments and quizzes to prepare for the upcoming test. You can benefit from studying with other students who have different learning and personality styles than yours, and the social interaction motivates you for the test.

75 Manage Your Testing Environment

In an online course, you will most likely take all of your tests online in your course LMS. This means you will probably be able to use your book and notes for the exam. Also, tests are usually timed, so you have a certain amount of time to complete the test. Depending on the instructor, you might have only one attempt at a test, or you might have more than one attempt.

As you prepare for your exam, you should organize your workspace and arrange your schedule so you have time to complete the test without interruption. The following are some things you can do to organize your testing environment:

- Remove clutter from your desk.
- Organize your notes.
- Have your textbook available and use sticky notes to mark important pages.
- Highlight important information in your textbook and notes.
- Get something to eat and drink and go to the bathroom before beginning the test.
- Relax and view the test as an opportunity to demonstrate your knowledge of the subject matter.

76 Read Instructions and Questions Carefully

Read the test instructions carefully and thoroughly before taking the test. The instructions provide specific details to guide you as you are taking the test. The following are some things to look for when reading instructions:

- How many questions are on the test?
- What types of questions are on the test?
- How long do I have to complete the test?
- How many attempts do I have on the test? Is there a delay between attempts?
- Do I have to complete the test once I start it, or can I save it and come back to it later?
- Are the results available immediately or after the due date?

There might be a variety of question types on each quiz: true/false, multiple choice, fill-in, short answer, or essay. Each of these different types of questions requires a different type of response from you. *Read each question carefully; don't just skim it.* On multiple choice questions, read all possible response choices before selecting an answer. Realize on multiple choice questions that some answer choices are "distractors;" distractors are potential responses that might distract you from the correct answer. On all questions, look for key words. Below is a list of key words to pay attention to:

- *True/false questions: always, never, all, none, sometimes, usually,* or *most*
- *Multiple choice questions: best answer* or *most correct choice*
- *Short answer and essay questions: summarize, evaluate, explain, compare, contrast, define,* or *discuss*

SHORT ANSWER AND ESSAY QUESTIONS

When responding to short answer or essay questions, use some of the writing strategies listed in #64–#70.

77 Pay Attention to Time

Before taking the test, make sure you know how much time you're allowed to complete the test. Usually when taking a test in an online environment (LMS), a timer is displayed that counts down the time you have remaining. Keep track of your time during the test. Before you begin, make sure that you have enough uninterrupted time to complete the test.

Some online tests display only one question at a time, while others display all of the questions at once. On some tests, you are able to go back and change a previous answer, while on others, you are not allowed to do this. The following are some good time management strategies:

- Answer easy questions first.
- Don't be afraid to skip questions and come back to them later (if that is an option).
- Go back through the test to make sure all questions are answered.
- Try to allow enough time to go back and review your answers.
- Proofread and edit essay and short answer responses.

78 Make Educated Guesses

Inevitably, you will encounter questions that you are not exactly sure of the answer. It is best to skip over these and come back to them later. Many times a subsequent question will trigger your memory or provide you with information to answer these previously skipped questions.

Always answer all of the questions. If you're not sure of the correct answer, respond with your best educated guess. On multiple choice questions, try to eliminate as many of the distractor and decoy responses as possible, and then make your best educated guess on the remaining choices. On essay and short answer questions, answer as much as you can; even partial credit or points on a question is better than leaving the question unanswered.

79 Have a Realistic View of the Test

Realize that each test you take is just a portion of your overall grade. If you don't do well on one test, this will not have a devastating effect on your overall grade and success in the course. But don't use this as an excuse for not preparing for a test. *Having a realistic view of the test makes you more relaxed and confident while taking the test, which reduces test anxiety and improves performance.* Also, remember that your value as an individual is not determined by your grade on a test.

80 Review Graded Tests

As soon as possible after the test, go back into your LMS and review the test. Sometimes test results are available immediately; sometimes they are available after the due date. For open-ended questions (fill-in, short answer, and essay), your professor will have to grade these questions manually. It might take a day or two for your professor to get these questions graded. So don't panic if you view your test results and have earned no points on these open-ended questions. Go back later and check your grade after your professor has had time to grade these questions.

Reviewing your tests helps you retain and recall information and learn from your mistakes. The only tragedy of a mistake on a test is not learning from it. Reviewing your tests also keeps you motivated throughout the course. If you did well, this motivates you to do well on subsequent assignments and tests. If you did not perform as well as you had hoped, this motivates you to be more diligent in your preparation before future tests.

PART 8: DO SOMETHING ABOUT IT

DISCUSS IT

8.1. Do you have more anxiety taking quizzes and tests in an online or on-site environment? What type of questions are most challenging for you? What are some of the things you do to reduce testing anxiety?

8.2. What are some techniques you use to prepare for a test? Why is it important to make educated guesses on questions? How does reviewing graded tests enhance learning?

8.3. How does managing your testing environment influence your performance on a test? Why is it important to read test instructions and questions carefully? What techniques do you use to manage time while taking a test?

WRITE IT

8.4. Preparing for a test is very important and helps to reduce test anxiety. Write a paragraph describing how you prepare for tests. Use writing techniques you learned in *Part 7: Writing Assignments* to improve the quality of your writing.

8.5. In a brief paragraph, explain in your own words why it is important to have a realistic view of each test, and how this influences both how you prepare for tests and how you perform on tests.

8.6. Use the Internet to look up test-taking strategies from at least three sources. Make a list of 10 different test-taking strategies and order them from most important to least important. List the names and URLs (web addresses) of the web sites where you found the information.

PART 9: WORKING IN GROUPS

For some of your online courses, you have group projects. Working in groups can be both rewarding and challenging. *In both your professional and personal life, the ability to work with others is essential.* Working in groups for an online course presents a unique set of challenges and opportunities, but many of the principles of working in groups is common to all types of courses. This section provides you with some useful tools when working in groups.

81 Get to Know Your Teammates

It is important to get to know the teammates who you will work closely with on a project. Getting to know your group members on a more personal level helps you appreciate them and work more effectively with them.

If all group members are fairly close in proximity, it is a good idea to meet for coffee to get to know each before beginning the project. If meeting together at a physical location is not an option, try scheduling a conference call or an online meeting. Before you begin working on the project, take some time to introduce yourselves and tell each other a little about yourselves. Without getting too personal, you can share some of the following:

> **ONLINE MEETING**
>
> Online video meetings can be done using Skype or ooVoo, which are both free online resources.

- Educational background and goals
- Family
- Interests (e.g., hobbies, activities, or sports; what would you most like to do with two free hours?)
- Goals for this group/project

82 Appoint a Project Leader

It is important to have a project leader serving as the point person for the group. The following are some of the possible duties of the project leader:

- Set meeting schedule.
- Prepare meeting agendas and action items.
- Email reminders.
- Assign tasks.
- Maintain a task list and group schedule.
- Follow up and provide accountability for action items.
- Communicate with the professor.
- Manage disagreements.

Choose a project leader who is organized and willing to take on additional responsibility. The ability to communicate well is a must. *A project leader does not necessarily have to do more work than the other team members, but rather the leader provides oversight and guidance to the process, progress, and success of the group.*

83 Communicate Effectively

Communication is one of the most important aspects of group work and directly contributes to the overall success of the group project. Use the following guidelines when communicating with your teammates:

- Communicate at least weekly with your teammates.
- Ask questions; feedback from your teammates will make your team stronger.
- Respond to emails from your teammates.
- Usually use *Reply to All* in your communication to keep all members "in the loop."
- Notify members early of problems that arise.
- Be very positive and encouraging in your communication.
- Use a phone call or conference call for more detailed information.

> **COMMUNICATING WITH TEAMMATES**
> See tips in *Part 3: Using Email* (beginning on page 12) to improve communication within your group.

84 Planning Your Project

When working on a project, there are three main components. Each of these three components takes approximately one-third of the total time of the project.

- *Planning and Research:* Brainstorming topics and subtopics, developing the problem and purpose, and researching the topic
- *Writing:* Writing the different sections of the report
- *Finalizing:* Proofreading, editing, and formatting

Be sure to give yourselves plenty of time to work on each of these three main areas. *Planning and research are the foundation on which an excellent report is built.* The better job you do planning and researching the report, the easier it is to write, and the better job you do writing the report, the easier it is to finalize the document.

85 Create Meeting Agendas

Before each meeting, whether in person or online, the project leader should create an agenda. *An agenda will help to guide discussion topics and manage time more effectively.* A week or so before the meeting, the project leader should send an email to the group asking for input about agenda topics. The project leader can include a tentative agenda and ask for other suggested topics of discussion. A couple of days before the meeting, the project leader should send out a meeting reminder email with meeting time, location, and duration details, and include the meeting agenda.

86 Create a Task List and Schedule

From each group meeting should flow a task list and a schedule. The *task list* provides details about the action items for which each group member is responsible. The *schedule* lists the due dates for the tasks. It is the responsibility of each group member to work diligently and complete his or her tasks by the due dates. It is the project leader's responsibility to monitor the task list and schedule to make sure the group is staying on schedule. A sample task list and schedule is shown below:

Task	Person (s) Responsible	Due Date
Problem and purpose statements	Randy & Kelly	Sept. 27
Concept map of main and subtopics	Karen & Rick	Oct. 1
Research for Section 1	Kelly	Oct. 9
Research for Section 2	Rick	Oct. 9
Research for Section 3	Randy	Oct. 9
Research for Section 4	Karen	Oct. 9

Notes:

5–8 sources of information for each section

Highlight and annotate pertinent info.

Format references in APA format

Next meeting Oct. 12, 7:30 p.m. conference call

87 Writing as a Team

ONLINE RESOURCES

See *Part 11: Using Online Resources* (beginning on page 54) for more information and links to these group-work resources.

When working on a group project or report, it is important that you not only write, proofread, and edit the sections that are your responsibility, but also proofread and edit others' writings. Each person has a different writing style, and, as a group, you need to produce a document that flows (similar in tone and style) from one section to the next.

Many LMSs have group work areas where you can share documents. There are also other free online resources such as *Wiggio, SkyDrive, SkyDrive Groups, Google Docs,* and *Dropbox,* which allow you to have an online storage area for groups and shared documents. You might consider using one of these resources to help facilitate the use of shared documents. Also, *Track Changes* and *Comments* in Microsoft Word are excellent tools when editing and commenting on your teammates' work.

88 Managing Conflict

Conflict is natural in interpersonal relationships. When working in groups, you might encounter conflict among team members. If this occurs, don't be afraid to deal with conflict. When managing conflict, it is best to do it face-to-face. If this is not possible, a phone or video call is the next best option. Avoid using email for conflict resolution because body language and voice tone, which communicate important information, are not present. The context of the conflict determines if the resolution needs to involve two or three individuals, or the entire group. The following are some tips to effectively deal with conflict:

- *Clarify the problem:* Try to get to the underlying issue of the conflict.
- *Make sure that a conflict exists:* Many times apparent conflict is a result of lack of communication.
- *Verify the accuracy of information:* When dealing with conflict, make sure that information from all parties is correct.
- *Use "I" statements rather than "you" statements:* "I" statements are less judgmental and tend to diffuse a conflict.
- *Look for positive alternatives and compromises:* Focus on what can be done rather than what can't be done.
- *Work to repair hurt feelings:* Take the initiative to restore respect and trust within the group.

If attempts at conflict resolution within your group are not successful, you should contact your professor. Your professor can function as a mediator to help your group work through conflict.

89 Finalizing a Project

After all of the time you and your group members have spent planning, researching, meeting, writing, and reviewing, you begin to see the light at the end of the tunnel. Finalizing your report or project is the final stage in this process, and it is an important one. When finalizing your project, you will focus on *content* and *correct and consistent format.*

Proofread to find spelling, grammar, and word usage errors. *Edit* to examine your document for content. Make sure your document flows from one section to the next. Make sure the main topics and subtopics relate back to the purpose of your report. It's best and easiest to write the introduction and conclusion after the entire body of the report has been written.

You also want to make sure your document is in the format required by your professor and the format is consistent throughout the document. Review the project instructions from your professor, paying particular attention to formatting (margins, font and size, spacing, page numbering, headings, and references). Review the entire document to ensure consistency.

PART 9: DO SOMETHING ABOUT IT

DISCUSS IT

9.1.   Describe your past experiences working in a group or on a team. Was it a positive or negative experience and why? What could you have done to make it a better group?

9.2.   What's the most challenging part when communicating within a group? What are some positive outcomes of good communication within a group? What can you do to enhance communication within your group?

9.3.   Describe a time when you mediated a conflict. What did you learn in this process? What could you have done better? What conflict management techniques have you learned from others?

WRITE IT

9.4.   Use the Internet to look up information on the stages of group development. Using your own words, write a paragraph or two summarizing the stages of group development.

9.5.   Reflect on someone in your life who has demonstrated positive leadership. Write a paragraph describing why you consider this person a good leader. Make a list of at least five leadership techniques you would use if you were appointed leader of a group.

9.6.   Use the Internet to look up conflict management techniques. Make a list of at least five conflict management techniques and provide a brief description of each. Make a list of at least three web sites (names and URLs) you can share with you professor and classmates.

PART 10: STAYING MOTIVATED THROUGHOUT THE COURSE

In study after study about student success in online courses, one of the key indicators of success is motivation. Staying motivated throughout the course is challenging but greatly contributes to success in your online course.

90 Set SMART Goals

Setting and achieving goals is essential to staying motivated. Most of us have goals such as "getting an education" or "obtaining a good job," but usually our goals are too general and lack specific outcomes. Setting SMART goals encourages you to be more detailed, which increases your chances of attaining your goals. The following list describes each aspect of a SMART goal:

- *Specific:* Answers What?

  What is the specific and detailed outcome(s) of your goal?

- *Measurable:* Answers "How?"

  How will you know when you achieve your goal?

- *Achievable:* Answers "Is this doable?"

  Is this goal realistic and achievable?

- *Relevant:* Answers "Why?"

  Why is this goal important to me?

- *Time-Related:* Answers "When?"

  When will I reach my goal?

A SMART goal addresses each of the above questions. The following examples show the difference between an in effective goal and well-written SMART goal:

- *Not a SMART goal*

  Complete my education in the next few years.

- *SMART goal*

  Complete my B.S. in Business Administration with an emphasis in Marketing by June 1, 2016, which will equip me with the knowledge needed to obtain an internship or entry-level position in marketing.

Some of your goals will be short term, while others will be more mid-range or long term. Larger goals can be broken into smaller goals to make them more achievable. You should set personal, educational, and professional goals for the following time frames:

- Within the next term (three to six months)
- one to two years
- three to five years

91 Discuss What You're Learning with Others

Including others in your learning and studies keeps you motivated. *Find friends, family members, or co-workers with whom you can share and discuss what you're learning in your courses.* This not only reinforces what you're learning, but also gives you a sense of accountability that will keep you motivated to continue to study hard and keep up with your course work.

92 Create Reward Incentives

Just like taking short breaks while you're studying helps you to remain focused, setting short-term goals and rewarding yourself for accomplishing these provides incentive to continue. At the beginning of the term set short-term and realistic goals. Reward yourself as you accomplish these goals.

These rewards can be as simple as a weekly night out with your spouse, friend, or significant other for making it through the week and completing all of your assignments. It doesn't have to be costly; it could be a bike ride or hike on Sunday afternoon. You can set up a special reward for scoring at or above a certain grade on an exam. Make a list of rewards that are special and motivate you, and then assign these to certain accomplishments in your course. *Rewards keep you motivated and working toward your larger goal of successfully completing your course.*

93 Review Your Accomplishments

Don't neglect to review what you have accomplished throughout the course don't wait until the end of the term to do this. *A few weeks into your course(s), look back and reflect upon what you've learned, assignments you've completed, and tests and quizzes you've taken.* Reward yourself for these accomplishments. Share these accomplishments with others. Continue to do this every few weeks throughout the term.

94 Connect with Your Classmates

Taking an online course can be somewhat isolating. Making contact and spending time with your classmates helps you feel more connected to others and motivated. If you live in close proximity, set up a study group or just a night out for coffee, dessert, or a drink. It's good to discuss your class and accomplishments with your classmates, but don't just limit discussion to your class. Enjoy the company and camaraderie of your classmates.

95 Take Initiative

In each of the areas discussed in this section, *take the initiative.* Don't wait for someone to ask you what you're learning or congratulate you on your successes in your course; initiate discussion about these topics. Take the initiative to get together with your classmates and reward yourself for your accomplishments. Taking initiative gives you control over your success and motivation.

96 Provide Time for Recreational Activities

It is absolutely essential that you include time in your schedule for some down time and recreational activities. Recreational activities actually "re-create" you and keep you energized and motivated throughout the term. Exercise is a great form of recreation that includes not only physical benefits but also mental benefits. You might also want to schedule time to hang out with friends and family, watch TV, go shopping, or play video games. *As you set up your weekly schedule and modify it throughout the term, be sure to schedule time for activities that refresh and rejuvenate you.*

PART 10: DO SOMETHING ABOUT IT

DISCUSS IT

10.1. Why is it more challenging to stay motivated during the last half of the course than at the beginning of the course? What do you do to stay motivated throughout the course?

10.2. Are you a goal setter? Why or why not? Why is it important to have goals? How do goals influence your performance in your courses?

10.3. How does connecting with you classmates help keep you motivated throughout the course? How does sharing with others what you're learning reinforce learning? How does reviewing past accomplishments influence motivation?

WRITE IT

10.4. Write three SMART goals: a personal goal, an educational goal, and a career goal. Each goal should address all five areas of a SMART goal.

10.5. Motivation throughout the course is difficult to maintain. Develop a plan to help you maintain your motivation level throughout the course, listing at least five different techniques, and describe how and when you will use each.

10.6. Write a paragraph describing how rewards can influence motivation. Make a list of at least three reward incentives and describe how each will be used.

PART 11: USING ONLINE RESOURCES

This section provides you with resources to support you in your online courses. Your professors, classmates, and counselors might also provide you with useful additional online resources.

97 Learning Resources

- *Purdue Online Writing Lab (OWL)*
  http://owl.english.purdue.edu/owl/

  A variety of writing resources that include not only general and research writing but also information about grammar, mechanics, and punctuation.

- *University of Chicago Writing Program*
  http://writing-program.uchicago.edu/resources/grammar.htm

  A clearinghouse of writing and grammar resources.

- *Math.com: The World of Math Online*
  http://www.math.com/

  Online resource for a variety of levels of mathematics.

- *Kahn Academy*
  https://www.khanacademy.org/

  Free online lectures and assessments on many different math, science, computer science, and humanities topics.

- *SQ3R*
  http://www.mindtools.com/pages/article/newISS_02.htm

  This method, *Survey, Question, Read, Recall,* and *Review,* provides an outline to improve study methods.

98 Free Software Resources

- *Office Web Apps and SkyDrive*
  https://skydrive.live.com

  Free online word processing, spreadsheet, presentation, notes, and survey programs. SkyDrive is free online storage. If you have a Microsoft account, you also have a SkyDrive account and access to Office Web Apps. You can also create SkyDrive groups and store and share documents in SkyDrive or SkyDrive Groups.

- *Google Drive and Docs*
  https://drive.google.com

  Free online word processing, spreadsheet, presentation, graphics, and forms programs and document storage. You must sign up for a free Google account to have access to Google Drive.

- *OpenOffice*
  http://www.openoffice.org/

  Open-source office software suite for word processing, spreadsheets, presentations, graphics, and databases.

- *Dropbox*
  https://www.dropbox.com/

  Free online storage where you can share files with others.

- *Wiggio*
  http://wiggio.com/

  Share and edit files, manage a group calendar, poll your group, post links, set up conference calls, chat online, and send mass texts, voice, and email messages to your group members.

- *Prezi*
  http://prezi.com/

  Cloud-based presentation software that is free for students and educators.

- *Picnik*
  http://www.picnik.com/

  Free, yet powerful, photo editing tool.

- *Slideshare*
  http://www.slideshare.net/

  Free online resource to share presentations, documents, and videos.

- *Jing*
  http://www.techsmith.com/jing/

  Free screen capture software to record screen snapshots, actions, and audio from your computer screen.

- *Screencast*
  http://screencast.com

  Online storage that can be used in conjunction with Jing to store screen captures and videos and share with others.

99 Education Discounts on Software

- *JourneyEd*
  http://www.journeyed.com/

  Academic pricing on Microsoft, Adobe, and other software for students, educators, and colleges.

- *College Buys*
  http://www.shopcollegebuys.org/

  Discounted pricing on Microsoft and Adobe products for California community college students.

- *Microsoft Store*
  http://www.microsoftstore.com

  Student discount pricing on Microsoft Office and Windows.

100 Software Training and Information

- *Microsoft Office help and tutorials*
  http://office.microsoft.com/en-us/support

- *Google Drive tutorials*
  https://support.google.com/drive/

- *OpenOffice tutorials*
  http://support.openoffice.org/

101 Other Online Resources

- *Free Application for Federal Student Aid (FAFSA)*
  http://www.fafsa.ed.gov/

  Online application and information about college scholarships.

- *Myers-Briggs Type Indicator*
  http://www.myersbriggs.org/

  Information about this personality indicator and how it can be applied to personal and professional life.

- *VARK Learning Styles*
  http://www.vark-learn.com

  Assessment and information about the different learning styles.

- *VisualCV*
  http://www.visualcv.com

  Create a free online resume and professional portfolio.

- *Skype*
  http://www.skype.com

  Free video calling through your computer and web camera.

- *ooVoo*
  http://www.oovoo.com

  Video conferencing that is free with three or fewer participants; a paid account allows up to 12 participants.

PART 11: DO SOMETHING ABOUT IT

DISCUSS IT

11.1. Which productivity software (e.g., Office, Google Docs, Office Web Apps, or Open Office) do you use and why do you use it? Have you tried others? When you don't know how to use a feature in the software, what do you do to learn how to use it?

11.2. Not including LMSs for your courses, what other online resources have you used? What online resources have been most beneficial to you and why? Are there online resources you would not recommend to your professors or classmates?

11.3. What free software do you use and which are your favorites? Have you used any of the software listed in *#98: Free Software Resources?* If so, which ones? Are there other free software or online resources you would recommend to you professors and classmates?

WRITE IT

11.4. Go to the VARK Learning Styles web site (*#101: Other Online Resources*) and take the questionnaire. After finishing the questionnaire, write a paragraph about your top two learning styles.

11.5. Go to the OWL web site (*#97: Learning Resources*) and look up information on either APA or MLA report styles. Write a list of at least eight features of the style and a description of each. Include information about report format, citations, and references.

11.6. Look up information about financial aid on your college's web site and the FAFSA web site (*#101: Other Online Resources*). Create a timeline of due dates for at least five different types of available financial aid. Using your own words, provide a description and what you need to do to apply for each of the different types of financial aid listed in your timeline.

PART 12: PROFESSIONAL PORTFOLIO, CONTACTS, MONTHLY CALENDAR, AND NOTES

Building Your Professional Portfolio

While you are attending college, you should begin to assemble a professional portfolio. Don't wait until you start looking for a career to put together your portfolio. Your professional portfolio is a fluid document that you regularly update and refine.

Purpose

The purpose of a professional portfolio is to showcase and document your skills, accomplishments, experience, and activities. Your portfolio is a reflection of who you are and provides documentation and samples of work beyond a resume or curriculum vitae.

A professional portfolio can be used in the following ways:

- Interviewing for a job
- Interviewing for a graduate education program
- Applying for a scholarship or internship
- Applying for a promotion
- Negotiating a raise

Content

The content of your professional portfolio varies depending on the purpose for which you are using it. A portfolio can be a comprehensive document highlighting a representative sample of your work, or it can be targeted for a specific purpose, such as applying for a community outreach grant or an educational scholarship.

Some of the general content in a professional portfolio includes:

- Professional statement (goals and philosophy)
- Resume or curriculum vitae
- Degrees and certifications
- Transcripts
- Letters of recommendation

Other more detailed and specific content might include:

- Writing samples
- College course projects
- Professional/educational organizations and activities

- Work project samples
- Evidence of leadership
- Awards and honors
- Published work
- Web sites
- Evaluations by professors or peers
- Performance reviews by supervisors
- Art, music, or video samples
- Photographs
- Conference presentation
- Volunteer service and experience

These lists are by no means exhaustive but can be used to help you brainstorm ideas for information to include in your portfolio. The contents of your professional portfolio are determined by your college major, experience, skills, and special talents. Include documents that demonstrate your diversity and the breadth and depth of your knowledge, skills, and experience.

Organization

You should organize your portfolio in a way that guides and educates the readers to form an accurate opinion about your qualifications and abilities.

1. Organize the contents in a binder.
2. Use dividers to categorize the information.
3. Include a title page that includes your name, address, telephone numbers, email address, web site URL, degree on which you are working, and anticipated graduation date.
4. Create a table of contents.
5. Explain supporting documentation. Use an introductory page to provide context for supporting documents.

Remember, your professional portfolio should be updated regularly to continually refine and reflect who you are. Regularly review your portfolio and reflect upon the contents. Ask yourself the following questions:

- Does it reflect and highlight my skills and accomplishments?
- Does it provide evidence of my abilities?
- Does it look professional?
- Can it be easily updated and targeted for a specific purpose?
- Does it guide the reader? Does it require additional explanation?

Finally, it is a good idea to keep both electronic and hard copies of your supporting documentation. Back up this information regularly.

ONLINE PORTFOLIOS

There are web sites that allow you to create an online professional portfolio. See *VisualCV* in *#101 Other Online Resources* on page 56.

Portfolio Checklist

Introductory documents
(title page, table of contents, and professional statement)

**Date/Date
Updated**

- ☐ _____ _____
- ☐ _____ _____
- ☐ _____ _____

Professional/Educational documents
(resume/curriculum vitae, degrees/certifications,
transcripts, and letters of recommendation)

- ☐ _____ _____
- ☐ _____ _____
- ☐ _____ _____
- ☐ _____ _____
- ☐ _____ _____
- ☐ _____ _____
- ☐ _____ _____
- ☐ _____ _____

Educational Accomplishments
(writing samples, professor and peer reviews, projects,
art work, web sites, student organizations, awards, etc.)

- ☐ _____ _____
- ☐ _____ _____
- ☐ _____ _____
- ☐ _____ _____
- ☐ _____ _____
- ☐ _____ _____
- ☐ _____ _____
- ☐ _____ _____

Professional Accomplishments
(work projects, supervisor reviews, professional
organizations, awards, conference participation, etc.)

- ☐ _____ _____
- ☐ _____ _____
- ☐ _____ _____
- ☐ _____ _____
- ☐ _____ _____
- ☐ _____ _____
- ☐ _____ _____
- ☐ _____ _____

Students and Group Members

NAME:

Address: _____
City, state, zip: _____
Cell phone: _____
Other phone: _____
Email 1: _____
Email 2: _____
Web site: _____
Facebook: _____
Twitter: _____
Other social network: _____
Birthday: _____
Other info.: _____
_____
_____

NAME:

Address: _____
City, state, zip: _____
Cell phone: _____
Other phone: _____
Email 1: _____
Email 2: _____
Web site: _____
Facebook: _____
Twitter: _____
Other social network: _____
Birthday: _____
Other info.: _____
_____
_____

NAME:

Address: _____
City, state, zip: _____
Cell phone: _____
Other phone: _____
Email 1: _____
Email 2: _____
Web site: _____
Facebook: _____
Twitter: _____
Other social network: _____
Birthday: _____
Other info.: _____
_____
_____

NAME:

Address: _____
City, state, zip: _____
Cell phone: _____
Other phone: _____
Email 1: _____
Email 2: _____
Web site: _____
Facebook: _____
Twitter: _____
Other social network: _____
Birthday: _____
Other info.: _____
_____
_____

NAME:

Address: _____
City, state, zip: _____
Cell phone: _____
Other phone: _____
Email 1: _____
Email 2: _____
Web site: _____
Facebook: _____
Twitter: _____
Other social network: _____
Birthday: _____
Other info.: _____
_____
_____

NAME:

Address: _____
City, state, zip: _____
Cell phone: _____
Other phone: _____
Email 1: _____
Email 2: _____
Web site: _____
Facebook: _____
Twitter: _____
Other social network: _____
Birthday: _____
Other info.: _____
_____
_____

Students and Group Members

NAME:

Address: _____
City, state, zip: _____
Cell phone: _____
Other phone: _____
Email 1: _____
Email 2: _____
Web site: _____
Facebook: _____
Twitter: _____
Other social network: _____
Birthday: _____
Other info.: _____
_____
_____

NAME:

Address: _____
City, state, zip: _____
Cell phone: _____
Other phone: _____
Email 1: _____
Email 2: _____
Web site: _____
Facebook: _____
Twitter: _____
Other social network: _____
Birthday: _____
Other info.: _____
_____
_____

NAME:

Address: _____
City, state, zip: _____
Cell phone: _____
Other phone: _____
Email 1: _____
Email 2: _____
Web site: _____
Facebook: _____
Twitter: _____
Other social network: _____
Birthday: _____
Other info.: _____
_____
_____

NAME:

Address: _____
City, state, zip: _____
Cell phone: _____
Other phone: _____
Email 1: _____
Email 2: _____
Web site: _____
Facebook: _____
Twitter: _____
Other social network: _____
Birthday: _____
Other info.: _____
_____
_____

NAME:

Address: _____
City, state, zip: _____
Cell phone: _____
Other phone: _____
Email 1: _____
Email 2: _____
Web site: _____
Facebook: _____
Twitter: _____
Other social network: _____
Birthday: _____
Other info.: _____
_____
_____

NAME:

Address: _____
City, state, zip: _____
Cell phone: _____
Other phone: _____
Email 1: _____
Email 2: _____
Web site: _____
Facebook: _____
Twitter: _____
Other social network: _____
Birthday: _____
Other info.: _____
_____
_____

Students and Group Members

NAME:
Address: _____
City, state, zip: _____
Cell phone: _____
Other phone: _____
Email 1: _____
Email 2: _____
Web site: _____
Facebook: _____
Twitter: _____
Other social network: _____
Birthday: _____
Other info.: _____
_____
_____

NAME:
Address: _____
City, state, zip: _____
Cell phone: _____
Other phone: _____
Email 1: _____
Email 2: _____
Web site: _____
Facebook: _____
Twitter: _____
Other social network: _____
Birthday: _____
Other info.: _____
_____
_____

NAME:
Address: _____
City, state, zip: _____
Cell phone: _____
Other phone: _____
Email 1: _____
Email 2: _____
Web site: _____
Facebook: _____
Twitter: _____
Other social network: _____
Birthday: _____
Other info.: _____
_____
_____

NAME:
Address: _____
City, state, zip: _____
Cell phone: _____
Other phone: _____
Email 1: _____
Email 2: _____
Web site: _____
Facebook: _____
Twitter: _____
Other social network: _____
Birthday: _____
Other info.: _____
_____
_____

NAME:
Address: _____
City, state, zip: _____
Cell phone: _____
Other phone: _____
Email 1: _____
Email 2: _____
Web site: _____
Facebook: _____
Twitter: _____
Other social network: _____
Birthday: _____
Other info.: _____
_____
_____

NAME:
Address: _____
City, state, zip: _____
Cell phone: _____
Other phone: _____
Email 1: _____
Email 2: _____
Web site: _____
Facebook: _____
Twitter: _____
Other social network: _____
Birthday: _____
Other info.: _____
_____
_____

Professors

NAME:
College: _____
Classes taken: _____
Address: _____
City, state, zip: _____
Phone: _____
Email 1: _____
Email 2: _____
Web site: _____
LinkedIn: _____
Twitter: _____
Other social network: _____
Birthday: _____
Other info.: _____
_____

NAME:
College: _____
Classes taken: _____
Address: _____
City, state, zip: _____
Phone: _____
Email 1: _____
Email 2: _____
Web site: _____
LinkedIn: _____
Twitter: _____
Other social network: _____
Birthday: _____
Other info.: _____
_____

NAME:
College: _____
Classes taken: _____
Address: _____
City, state, zip: _____
Phone: _____
Email 1: _____
Email 2: _____
Web site: _____
LinkedIn: _____
Twitter: _____
Other social network: _____
Birthday: _____
Other info.: _____
_____

NAME:
College: _____
Classes taken: _____
Address: _____
City, state, zip: _____
Phone: _____
Email 1: _____
Email 2: _____
Web site: _____
LinkedIn: _____
Twitter: _____
Other social network: _____
Birthday: _____
Other info.: _____
_____

NAME:
College: _____
Classes taken: _____
Address: _____
City, state, zip: _____
Phone: _____
Email 1: _____
Email 2: _____
Web site: _____
LinkedIn: _____
Twitter: _____
Other social network: _____
Birthday: _____
Other info.: _____
_____

NAME:
College: _____
Classes taken: _____
Address: _____
City, state, zip: _____
Phone: _____
Email 1: _____
Email 2: _____
Web site: _____
LinkedIn: _____
Twitter: _____
Other social network: _____
Birthday: _____
Other info.: _____
_____

Professors

| **NAME:** |
| College: _____ |
| Classes taken: _____ |
| Address: _____ |
| City, state, zip: _____ |
| Phone: _____ |
| Email 1: _____ |
| Email 2: _____ |
| Web site: _____ |
| LinkedIn: _____ |
| Twitter: _____ |
| Other social network: _____ |
| Birthday: _____ |
| Other info.: _____ |
| _____ |

NAME:
College: _____
Classes taken: _____
Address: _____
City, state, zip: _____
Phone: _____
Email 1: _____
Email 2: _____
Web site: _____
LinkedIn: _____
Twitter: _____
Other social network: _____
Birthday: _____
Other info.: _____
_____

NAME:
College: _____
Classes taken: _____
Address: _____
City, state, zip: _____
Phone: _____
Email 1: _____
Email 2: _____
Web site: _____
LinkedIn: _____
Twitter: _____
Other social network: _____
Birthday: _____
Other info.: _____
_____

NAME:
College: _____
Classes taken: _____
Address: _____
City, state, zip: _____
Phone: _____
Email 1: _____
Email 2: _____
Web site: _____
LinkedIn: _____
Twitter: _____
Other social network: _____
Birthday: _____
Other info.: _____
_____

NAME:
College: _____
Classes taken: _____
Address: _____
City, state, zip: _____
Phone: _____
Email 1: _____
Email 2: _____
Web site: _____
LinkedIn: _____
Twitter: _____
Other social network: _____
Birthday: _____
Other info.: _____
_____

NAME:
College: _____
Classes taken: _____
Address: _____
City, state, zip: _____
Phone: _____
Email 1: _____
Email 2: _____
Web site: _____
LinkedIn: _____
Twitter: _____
Other social network: _____
Birthday: _____
Other info.: _____
_____

Professors

NAME:

College: _____

Classes taken: _____

Address: _____

City, state, zip: _____

Phone: _____

Email 1: _____

Email 2: _____

Web site: _____

LinkedIn: _____

Twitter: _____

Other social network: _____

Birthday: _____

Other info.: _____

_____

NAME:

College: _____

Classes taken: _____

Address: _____

City, state, zip: _____

Phone: _____

Email 1: _____

Email 2: _____

Web site: _____

LinkedIn: _____

Twitter: _____

Other social network: _____

Birthday: _____

Other info.: _____

_____

NAME:

College: _____

Classes taken: _____

Address: _____

City, state, zip: _____

Phone: _____

Email 1: _____

Email 2: _____

Web site: _____

LinkedIn: _____

Twitter: _____

Other social network: _____

Birthday: _____

Other info.: _____

_____

NAME:

College: _____

Classes taken: _____

Address: _____

City, state, zip: _____

Phone: _____

Email 1: _____

Email 2: _____

Web site: _____

LinkedIn: _____

Twitter: _____

Other social network: _____

Birthday: _____

Other info.: _____

_____

NAME:

College: _____

Classes taken: _____

Address: _____

City, state, zip: _____

Phone: _____

Email 1: _____

Email 2: _____

Web site: _____

LinkedIn: _____

Twitter: _____

Other social network: _____

Birthday: _____

Other info.: _____

_____

NAME:

College: _____

Classes taken: _____

Address: _____

City, state, zip: _____

Phone: _____

Email 1: _____

Email 2: _____

Web site: _____

LinkedIn: _____

Twitter: _____

Other social network: _____

Birthday: _____

Other info.: _____

_____

Professional and Networking Contacts

NAME:

Title: _____
Company: _____
Address: _____
City, state, zip: _____
Cell phone: _____
Office phone: _____
Email 1: _____
Email 2: _____
Web site: _____
LinkedIn: _____
Facebook: _____
Twitter: _____
Other social network: _____
Birthday: _____
Other info.: _____
_____
_____

☐ Reference letter
☐ Job reference
☐ Employer/former employer
☐ Job contact
☐ Information interview

NAME:

Title: _____
Company: _____
Address: _____
City, state, zip: _____
Cell phone: _____
Office phone: _____
Email 1: _____
Email 2: _____
Web site: _____
LinkedIn: _____
Facebook: _____
Twitter: _____
Other social network: _____
Birthday: _____
Other info.: _____
_____
_____

☐ Reference letter
☐ Job reference
☐ Employer/former employer
☐ Job contact
☐ Information interview

NAME:

Title: _____
Company: _____
Address: _____
City, state, zip: _____
Cell phone: _____
Office phone: _____
Email 1: _____
Email 2: _____
Web site: _____
LinkedIn: _____
Facebook: _____
Twitter: _____
Other social network: _____
Birthday: _____
Other info.: _____
_____
_____

☐ Reference letter
☐ Job reference
☐ Employer/former employer
☐ Job contact
☐ Information interview

NAME:

Title: _____
Company: _____
Address: _____
City, state, zip: _____
Cell phone: _____
Office phone: _____
Email 1: _____
Email 2: _____
Web site: _____
LinkedIn: _____
Facebook: _____
Twitter: _____
Other social network: _____
Birthday: _____
Other info.: _____
_____
_____

☐ Reference letter
☐ Job reference
☐ Employer/former employer
☐ Job contact
☐ Information interview

Professional and Networking Contacts

NAME:

Title: _____
Company: _____
Address: _____
City, state, zip: _____
Cell phone: _____
Office phone: _____
Email 1: _____
Email 2: _____
Web site: _____
LinkedIn: _____
Facebook: _____
Twitter: _____
Other social network: _____
Birthday: _____
Other info.: _____
_____
_____

☐ Reference letter
☐ Job reference
☐ Employer/former employer
☐ Job contact
☐ Information interview

NAME:

Title: _____
Company: _____
Address: _____
City, state, zip: _____
Cell phone: _____
Office phone: _____
Email 1: _____
Email 2: _____
Web site: _____
LinkedIn: _____
Facebook: _____
Twitter: _____
Other social network: _____
Birthday: _____
Other info.: _____
_____
_____

☐ Reference letter
☐ Job reference
☐ Employer/former employer
☐ Job contact
☐ Information interview

NAME:

Title: _____
Company: _____
Address: _____
City, state, zip: _____
Cell phone: _____
Office phone: _____
Email 1: _____
Email 2: _____
Web site: _____
LinkedIn: _____
Facebook: _____
Twitter: _____
Other social network: _____
Birthday: _____
Other info.: _____
_____
_____

☐ Reference letter
☐ Job reference
☐ Employer/former employer
☐ Job contact
☐ Information interview

NAME:

Title: _____
Company: _____
Address: _____
City, state, zip: _____
Cell phone: _____
Office phone: _____
Email 1: _____
Email 2: _____
Web site: _____
LinkedIn: _____
Facebook: _____
Twitter: _____
Other social network: _____
Birthday: _____
Other info.: _____
_____
_____

☐ Reference letter
☐ Job reference
☐ Employer/former employer
☐ Job contact
☐ Information interview

Professional and Networking Contacts

NAME:

Title: _____

Company: _____

Address: _____

City, state, zip: _____

Cell phone: _____

Office phone: _____

Email 1: _____

Email 2: _____

Web site: _____

LinkedIn: _____

Facebook: _____

Twitter: _____

Other social network: _____

Birthday: _____

Other info.: _____

_____

☐ Reference letter
☐ Job reference
☐ Employer/former employer
☐ Job contact
☐ Information interview

NAME:

Title: _____

Company: _____

Address: _____

City, state, zip: _____

Cell phone: _____

Office phone: _____

Email 1: _____

Email 2: _____

Web site: _____

LinkedIn: _____

Facebook: _____

Twitter: _____

Other social network: _____

Birthday: _____

Other info.: _____

_____

☐ Reference letter
☐ Job reference
☐ Employer/former employer
☐ Job contact
☐ Information interview

NAME:

Title: _____

Company: _____

Address: _____

City, state, zip: _____

Cell phone: _____

Office phone: _____

Email 1: _____

Email 2: _____

Web site: _____

LinkedIn: _____

Facebook: _____

Twitter: _____

Other social network: _____

Birthday: _____

Other info.: _____

_____

☐ Reference letter
☐ Job reference
☐ Employer/former employer
☐ Job contact
☐ Information interview

NAME:

Title: _____

Company: _____

Address: _____

City, state, zip: _____

Cell phone: _____

Office phone: _____

Email 1: _____

Email 2: _____

Web site: _____

LinkedIn: _____

Facebook: _____

Twitter: _____

Other social network: _____

Birthday: _____

Other info.: _____

_____

☐ Reference letter
☐ Job reference
☐ Employer/former employer
☐ Job contact
☐ Information interview

MONTH _____

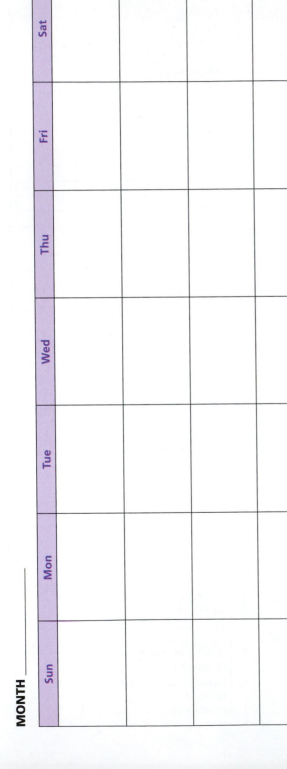

MONTH _____

Sun	Mon	Tue	Wed	Thu	Fri	Sat

MONTH _____

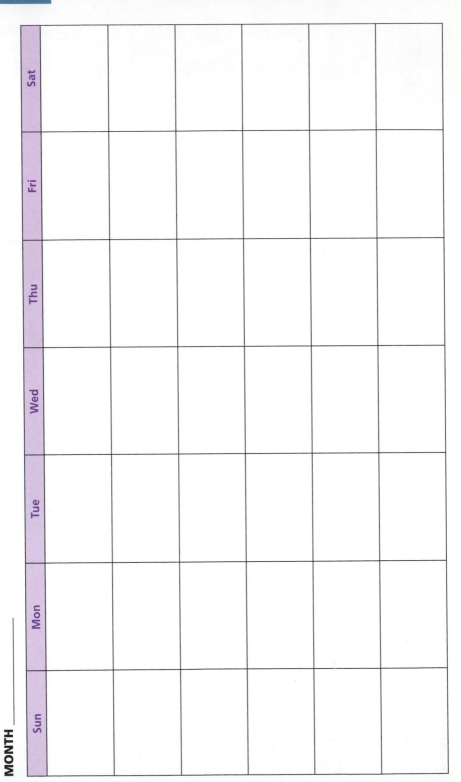

Sun	Mon	Tue	Wed	Thu	Fri	Sat

MONTH _____

Sun	Mon	Tue	Wed	Thu	Fri	Sat

MONTH _____

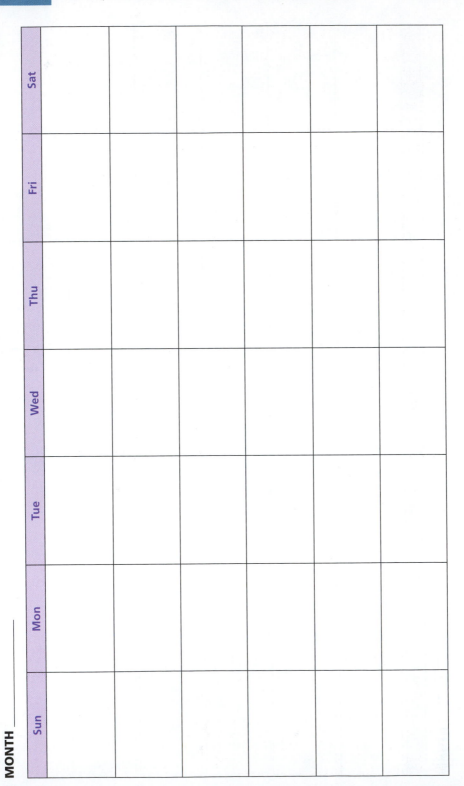

MONTH _____

Sun	Mon	Tue	Wed	Thu	Fri	Sat

MONTH _____

Sun	Mon	Tue	Wed	Thu	Fri	Sat

MONTH _____

Sun	Mon	Tue	Wed	Thu	Fri	Sat

MONTH _____

Sun	Mon	Tue	Wed	Thu	Fri	Sat

MONTH _____

Sun	Mon	Tue	Wed	Thu	Fri	Sat

MONTH _____

Sun	Mon	Tue	Wed	Thu	Fri	Sat

MONTH _____

Sun	Mon	Tue	Wed	Thu	Fri	Sat

MONTH _____

Sun	Mon	Tue	Wed	Thu	Fri	Sat

MONTH _____

Sun	Mon	Tue	Wed	Thu	Fri	Sat

MONTH

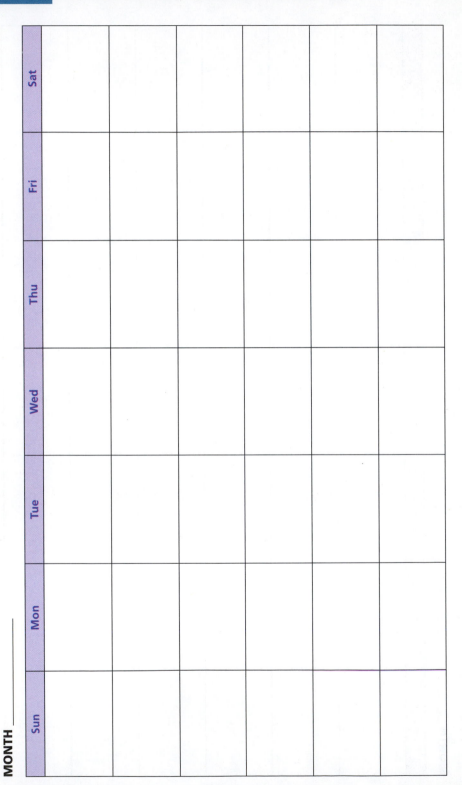

MONTH _____

Sun	Mon	Tue	Wed	Thu	Fri	Sat

MONTH _____

Sun	Mon	Tue	Wed	Thu	Fri	Sat

MONTH _____

Sun	Mon	Tue	Wed	Thu	Fri	Sat

Notes